PATSY'S
COOKBOOK

To Rose,
HAPPY Birthday. Bon Appetito
Enjoy The book. All the best.
God Bless
Sal J. Scognamillo

PATSY'S

COOKBOOK

CLASSIC ITALIAN RECIPES

from a

NEW YORK CITY
LANDMARK
RESTAURANT

Sal J. Scognamillo

foreword by

NANCY SINATRA

CLARKSON POTTER/PUBLISHERS
NEW YORK

Published by Clarkson Potter/Publishers, New York, New York.
Member of the Crown Publishing Group, a division of Random House, Inc.
www.randomhouse.com
www.patsys.com

CLARKSON N. POTTER is a trademark and POTTER and colophon are registered
trademarks of Random House, Inc.

Printed in the United States of America

Design by Jane Treuhaft

Library of Congress Cataloging-in-Publication Data
Scognamillo, Sal
    Patsy's cookbook : classic Italian recipes from a New York City landmark
    restaurant / Sal Scognamillo.
        Includes index.
        1. Cookery, Italian.   2. Patsy's (Restaurant)   I. Title.
TX723 .S3667   2002
    641.5945—dc21   2001054852

    ISBN 0-609-60954-8

    10   9   8   7   6   5   4   3   2   1

    First Edition

When we told our customers that we had finally decided to follow their suggestions and that we were, indeed, writing a book, many of them said they wanted to be part of our project. They had things they wanted to say about the restaurant and us. We are happy to include their comments, and we thank them for their contributions.

That's why we want to dedicate this book, first of all, to my grandparents, Pasquale and Concetta, and next, to our friends—all the people who dine here with us at Patsy's. *Grazie tanto.*

Patsy's

ITALIAN RESTAURANT

SOUVENIR MENU

236 WEST 56TH STREET
NEW YORK CITY
TEL. CIRCLE 7-3491

CONTENTS

FOREWORD BY NANCY SINATRA

My father absolutely loved Patsy's Italian Restaurant. The Scognamillo family dynasty is not unlike the Sinatras'. Theirs is in food and ours is in music, but the same kind of passion and love for the family business is required for success in either field.

If you visit New York looking for a special place that will make you feel at home, that's Patsy's. If you live in New York, do you have a hangout that welcomes you when you are alone, hungry, in need of friendly faces? That's Patsy's. Considering the thousands of bistros and brasseries in the Big Apple, odds are that many people will not hear about this wonderful place. The Scognamillo family doesn't need to publicize their prize, because the chairs are filled every day and every night by those fortunate enough to know of it through word of mouth. The proprietors and the menu speak volumes about its qualities without any fanfare. No bragging is necessary.

Beginning with Patsy himself, who was a loving, soft-spoken gentleman, the family is generous of spirit. Patsy was a man small in stature but gigantic in culinary artistry. He was old-fashioned in the best sense. His old-world way of making his patrons feel at home was, for me, just like visiting my own grandparents. He was a sweet, dear man who, though he seldom came out of the kitchen, occasionally walked into the dining room, checking to see if everybody was happy. I can still see him in my mind's eye, in his apron, his dark-rimmed eyeglasses with the sweet eyes behind them, looking questioningly around the room for a sign of dissatisfaction, but hoping not to find any. I think he was a little shy about his broken English. If his customer spoke Italian, as my father did (a little), he was able to converse very well. For the rest of us, his best communication was through the delicious food and warm hugs.

Patsy's natural passion and friendliness were reflected in the home-cooking kind of recipes he prepared. From the antipasti to the cannoli, he put his heart into every item on the menu. One of the specialties of the house—and one of the dishes I crave when I'm away from New York—is the zucchini with olive oil and garlic.

I remember the first time I went to Patsy's. I was a teenager, invited there by Father Robert Perella. Known as the Show Business Priest, Father Bob was a fixture in Manhattan. He was great fun to be with and knew the good eateries. We sat upstairs and enjoyed a wonderful meal.

Of course, I went to Patsy's many times (I couldn't possibly count the number) with my father over the years. We had some great family celebrations there as well as casual dinners and after-theater suppers. My dad always said, "When you go to a new Italian restaurant, you should always try pasta with tomato sauce first. If the sauce isn't good, the rest of the food won't be either." My favorite of the tomato sauces at Patsy's is the spicy Fra Diavolo. Joe also opened the place for lunch, and I began to have some of my business meetings there over a bowl of linguine or a nice piece of striped bass. Sometimes I think the food helped secure the deals!

When Patsy retired to Florida, we were a little concerned about whether or not the restaurant would remain the same. We knew Joe and Anna, Patsy's kids, but without Patsy? We needn't have worried. Family pride prevailed. They took over, and without a hitch the restaurant carried on. I must say that I was sad not to see Patsy there anymore, but we were happy that he had chosen to spend his last years relaxing and enjoying himself.

With Frank DiCola at the door and Joey in the kitchen, things were as warm and delicious as ever. Joey's wife, Rose, and his sister, Anna, made guests feel so welcome as they entered, or with their sweet voices on the telephone. The captains, the waiters, and the busboys all reflected the spirit of the family. If they knew you, they would anticipate your desires and see to them before you even asked.

The place was never better than when Joey took over the running of it. A natural host, he was born to do this. Under his leadership, Patsy's packaged products were sent to the marketplace and are now for sale, which is no small accomplishment. I order mine online.

The younger Scognamillos, Patsy's grandchildren, took their place in the family business. Joey's son, Sal, and Anna's son, Frank, began to take on more and more responsibilities at the restaurant. With Frankie hosting up front and Sal learning the ropes in the kitchen, the power was shifting, but the quality remained the same. And when we heard the sad news that Patsy had passed away, it was as though we had lost one of our own family members.

The Scognamillos and the Sinatras are as one family. My children, now on their own, are regular customers. It represents home to all of us. When I am away from the city for too long, I have to come up with a reason to go to New York, just to get my Patsy's fix. I have been known to race to the restaurant from JFK or Penn Station, luggage and all, before going to the hotel. Meanwhile, back in Los Angeles, I keep a supply of Patsy's sauces and other products in my kitchen.

Patsy's is more than a restaurant. To me it is a touchstone. I have so many sentimental memories—images of my grandparents, my mother, sister, brother, and children. The picture of my father, upstairs at a huge table, showing his granddaughters how to make a rocket from the cookie wrapper by rolling it into a cylinder and setting a match to it, delights me—my children's bright faces grinning at their impish grandpa. I can picture friends like Frank Military, Sonny Golden, Dad's cousin Buddy Garavente, Ava Gardner, Tony Bennett, Rosemary Clooney, Jilly Rizzo, and Mia Farrow and her children, sitting at the small table by the stairs, or the long table behind the bar. These, and countless others, are precious, vivid moments, poignantly etched in my heart forever. What a gift!

PREFACE

Patsy's Restaurant has been a New York City favorite at its only location on Fifty-sixth Street for nearly sixty years. It was first opened in 1944 by my grandfather Pasquale Scognamillo and my grandmother Concetta. My grandparents had arrived from Naples in the early twenties, and it was the immigration officials on Ellis Island who shortened Pasquale to Patsy. Emigrating to the United States hadn't been easy for them. My grandfather had to go to Cuba first, where he took whatever work he could find until he could come to the United States. Once in New York, he worked a variety of jobs and saved enough money to be able to send for my grandmother and my aunt Anna.

It took fourteen years, with everyone working very hard—that includes his children, Joe (my father) and Anna—before my grandfather had the money to open his first restaurant, the Sorrento, on West Forty-ninth Street. How and why Patsy's has outlasted so many restaurants in a city where restaurants appear and disappear with the speed of light, is, I think, due to our family, and to the fact that we never expanded and concentrated all our efforts on one restaurant.

Three generations of Scognamillos have created a very special landscape at Patsy's, and there have been only three master chefs at our restaurant: my grandfather Patsy; my father, Joe; and me. None of us went to cooking school—not that there's anything wrong with a cooking school. But our lessons were more personal, handed down from father to son to grandson (me). My father says we did go to school—the school of hard knocks. Nothing can compare with the hands-on lessons you learn when you work with your father and you start out doing the simplest, most menial tasks in the kitchen. Work your way up gradually, and you really learn what makes a restaurant work.

My father and I have tried to stay true to the original Neapolitan recipes of my grandfather, and we've never deviated from the philosophy that our customers come first.

Because of that, we're always willing to custom-tailor a recipe for a patron. We've never denied that ours is a "red-sauce restaurant"; we're proud of it. My father learned from his father that dishes from southern Italy could be every bit as elegant and certainly as delicious as dishes from the north. Flavor and finesse, I learned early on, do not disappear when you travel south of Rome.

Is there a secret to our cooking? No secret, just a home truth: Our sauces, red and otherwise, and all the other dishes on our menu are prepared with the best ingredients and truly loving care. And we are consistent. We don't change a recipe just to satisfy a trend. As one of our customers said, "I've been eating Patsy's Clams Posillipo for twenty years. It's a great dish, and I expect it to taste the same whenever I order it. I hope they never change the recipe to incorporate some new Asian spice." No chance of that. We let other places go fusion one year and Mediterranean the next. We're proud of Grandfather Patsy's recipes and we stay with them. Like our Chopped Salad, which seems newly popular today but was created by my grandfather in 1946 and has had its place on our menu since then.

PATSY'S

COOKBOOK

FS

December, 1994

Dear Joe, Frank and Sal!

Thank you so much for thinking of us at the holidays with the pasta sauce! It's great and we will all enjoy it over the holidays! Barbara and I truly appreciate your thinking of us and we send you ALL our love.

With warmest regards,

Frank Sinatra

Frank Sinatra

George Kalinsky

INTRODUCTION THE INSIDE STORY:
PATSY'S AND FRANK SINATRA

"We met Frank Sinatra in 1942," says Aunt Anna. "He was at the Paramount, and he was brought in to our restaurant by the Dorsey Brothers—the bandleaders Jimmy and Tommy. He fell in love with our whole family, and we loved him right back. When my mother was busy, he would answer the phone, take reservations, mix drinks.

"Later on he would come in with his wife, Nancy, and their three kids, Nancy, Tina, and Frank Jr. If he had a friend or knew a celebrity, you could be sure that he would bring them to Patsy's. Way before his Rat Pack—Dean Martin, Sammy Davis Jr., Joey Bishop—he came in with Milton Berle, Frank McHugh, Pat O'Brien. He gave Jimmy Cagney and his wife a big anniversary party at our restaurant. He knew everyone—and everyone wanted to know him. He introduced Governor Hugh Carey to Patsy's, and one night he showed up with the first three astronauts.

"The people on our Wall of Fame are somewhat like a family tree. Frank Sinatra brought in many people: Sammy Davis Jr., for example. Jackie Gleason brought in Tom Hanks. Rosemary Clooney brought in her brother, Nick, who brought in his son George Clooney. One of our closest friends, Rush Limbaugh, was brought in by Roger Ailes, and I just can't begin to list all the people Rush brought to Patsy's—including many people from his studio audience when he would announce that he was coming to our restaurant that day.

"What did Frank like to eat? Lots of things. Sometimes he went into the kitchen and helped Sal cook. Among his favorite dishes were Clams Posillipo (he could eat three orders of that), Chicken Piccata, and Veal Cutlets sliced really thin and fried until they were crisp. He liked sausages, and meatballs made only with veal. He loved our desserts: Pasticiotto was a big favorite (that's a lemon custard tart, and he had it topped with vanilla ice cream), Sfogliatelle, Cannoli. And whatever was left on the dessert cart he would take home and have for breakfast the next day.

"People still come here because of Frank, especially people in the music business. Bono of that Irish rock band U2 came in and said he wanted to eat at Patsy's because Frank Sinatra had told him it was his favorite place. I have to admit that neither I nor my son, Frank, knew who Bono was. Frank asked him if he was related to Sonny Bono. And Roger Daltrey of the Who came and asked Joe if it was true that a lot of famous people came to Patsy's because of Frank. Joe pointed to a table where Tony Bennett was sitting and said, 'Go ask him.' Roger did just that, and Tony answered, 'Just remember that this is Frank Sinatra's favorite place. This is his world, and we're all only living in it.'

"I know that our family certainly continues to live in his world. We have so many good memories of Frank, and one of my favorites is when Frank gave a dinner for thirty people and asked his guests to rise and toast my brother Joe. He was a special friend to all of us at Patsy's."

SAMMY DAVIS JR. GIVES A PARTY

"Sammy Davis Jr. often gave parties at Patsy's and I remember one time when he called and said he wanted to give a party at Patsy's for about forty people," says Joe. "I took the reservation and told Sammy I would arrange everything.

"The next thing I knew Frank Sinatra called—he had just come back from a European tour—and said *he* wanted to give a party on the same night, also for around forty people. I didn't know what to do. Sammy and Frank both wanted the upstairs room for a private party, and it's just not big enough to hold two parties of forty people each.

"I told Frank about Sammy's call and he said, 'Don't worry, Joey, I'll fix things. Just arrange the room for one party of forty. Everything's going to be okay.'

"The night of the party, I didn't know who or what to expect. But we arranged the room for one party of forty and waited. About nine o'clock, Sammy arrived followed by his guests.

"'Is Frank coming?' I asked.

"'Nah,' said Sammy. 'We tossed for who would get to eat at Patsy's tonight, and Frank lost the toss.'"

"Frank Sinatra and Sammy Davis Jr. were close friends, and whenever they were in New York together they would hang out at Patsy's. One night, sitting upstairs at their usual table with other friends, they were playing this game of 'anything you can do, I can do better'—an exercise in one-upmanship that went on for maybe twenty minutes. First Frank announced that he was a better dancer than Sammy. He got up and did a soft-shoe tap, gave a little bow, and indicated that it was Sammy's turn. So Sammy did a tap routine, and said, 'If you're a better dancer than I am, then I'm a better singer than you are.' He started singing 'New York, New York.'

"Frank laughed, and before Sammy finished singing, Frank was singing with him, and then over him, and the last long-held note was Frank's.

"At the end of the note, Sammy reached into one eye socket, pulled out his glass eye, and slammed it on the table. 'Okay, Mr. Chairman, can you top this?'

"Frank Sinatra was laughing, as was everyone at the table. 'That's it, Pal,' Frank said, raising his glass to Sammy. 'You've definitely got the last word.'"

FRANK AND THE ONLY TIME HE DIDN'T PICK UP THE CHECK

"Frank Sinatra was the biggest check grabber I ever knew," says Joe. "Whenever he ate at Patsy's, he was the host and everyone else was the guest. He insisted upon it. That's why I was surprised one day when he called to say he would be coming to dinner with a man and his wife, and that it was okay for me to give the check to the other man.

"I guess I sounded surprised when he told me that, and he said, 'Tonight I'm going to be the guest, Joey. But I want you to take care of me as always, so stay close—don't be more than four feet away from me. Okay?'

"Of course, anything that Frank wanted was okay with me. Frank and his wife, Barbara, arrived first and went upstairs to Frank's usual table. About fifteen minutes later, Frank's friends, a well-dressed couple, arrived and joined Frank and Barbara. I didn't recognize them, but they said a warm hello, and the four had a nice, leisurely dinner that took maybe three hours.

"I guess it was close to eleven when the man asked for the check. I looked over at Frank and he gave me a little nod, and I handed the other man the check. He didn't bother to look at it, just took out a Platinum American Express card and handed it to me.

"I went downstairs and gave the card to the cashier, and then went back up to see if there was anything else that Frank and his friends wanted. A few minutes later the waiter came up and signaled to me.

"'What?' I asked.

"'Can I see you downstairs for a minute?' the waiter asked. The waiter told me that the man's American Express card had been denied.

"'Can't be,' I said.

"'You try it,' the waiter told me.

"I put the card in the machine to process it, and sure enough, it came up 'denied.' I tried it one more time, and again, 'denied.'

"When that happens, the thing to do is to call the credit card company, so I called American Express. The woman at the other end asked me to wait a minute, and then she said. 'That card has been denied. How many times do we have to tell you people that?'

"What to do? I didn't want to embarrass Frank's guests, so I went upstairs and did the only thing I could think of doing. I returned the card to the man and said, 'I'd like you to be my guests tonight.'

"The man looked surprised, but Frank just wouldn't let that go. 'Joey, is this some kind of a joke? What's wrong?'

"'Nothing,' I said. 'Just forget it, Frank.'

"'No way,' Frank said. 'What's the matter?'

"I hated to explain in front of everyone, but with Frank insisting I finally said, 'Sorry, but this gentleman's card has been denied.'

"Frank started to laugh as though I had just told the funniest joke in the world. But the man got really mad. 'What? My card has been denied—*my* card? You better show me that.'

"So he came downstairs with me and I processed his card again. And once again the word *denied* came up.

"'Get them on the phone for me, Joe,' he said, 'and then let me talk to them.'

"So I dialed the number, got American Express, heard once more that the card had been denied, and put Frank's friend on the phone. He asked the woman to confirm what she had told me, that his card had been denied. And then he asked her name.

PATSY'S *Wall of Fame*

It started in 1944 when my grandfather opened Patsy's Italian Restaurant on West Fifty-sixth Street. From the beginning, the Broadway showbiz crowd thronged to the restaurant. It didn't take long for my grandfather to realize that he had a unique clientele: young Frank Sinatra, the Dorsey Brothers, and Rosemary Clooney, when she was just starting out. They said things to my grandfather like, "Coming here makes me feel at home," and, "The food is great, and you and your wife are even greater."

My grandfather truly liked his customers, and they became like family. And, like anyone who has a family, he wanted their pictures to remember them by. That's how our Wall of Fame started—my grandfather asked his customers for their pictures, and he also asked them to write a few words.

It didn't take long for the Wall of Fame to grow. Come to Patsy's today and you'll see some great shots of Jackie Gleason, James Cagney, Tom Hanks, Carl Reiner, Mario Lanza, Burt Lancaster, Lou Costello, and George Clooney. Do you have a favorite actor or singer? I'll bet you'll find their picture on our wall.

And when you look at the pictures, you'll be able to read what many of them wrote about our restaurant: "We love you, Patsy and Concetta." "Joe and Anna, you're terrific! Patsy would be proud of you." "When I'm in New York, I always make my pasta pilgrimage to Patsy's." And "Sal, I really miss you and your Clams Posillipo when I'm in Hollywood."

Whether it was Burt Reynolds or Lou Duva, Debbie Reynolds or Dom DeLuise, Gene Kelly or Kaye Ballard, they all expressed the same sentiments—our food is great, but even more important, we make everyone feel like they're part of the family. We've been told that the warmth and TLC we offer is rare in fast-paced New York.

And while we enjoy our starry clientele (one of our customers said they twinkle) we feel that all of our guests are celebrities. You don't have to be a Tony Bennett or a Rudy Giuliani to get good service and great food at Patsy's. Every one of our customers is a special star to us.

"Frank's friend said, 'You know that chair you're sitting on? It's mine. And that desk you're sitting at? That's mine, too. And that phone you're holding? That belongs to me. This is James Robinson speaking. And I hope you recognize the name, because I'm the president of American Express. Now, perhaps you'd like to check the numbers on that card again. No, don't talk to me about computer error. American Express doesn't make computer errors. You'll hear from my office in the morning.'

"Frank had come downstairs by that time, and was listening to Mr. Robinson and laughing. 'Don't fire her, Jim,' he said. 'I haven't had such a good laugh in months.'

"That's what happened the only time Frank ever let anybody else pick up a check."

FRANK, BILLY MARTIN, AND THE YANKEES

"It was the year the Yankees won the World Series when Billy Martin was the manager," says Joe. "I got a call asking me to reserve a table upstairs for forty-eight people—the Yankees were coming to celebrate at Patsy's.

"When Billy Martin and the rest of the Yankees arrived, I took them upstairs. But I didn't give them their usual table—the one in the alcove and behind a curtain for maximum privacy.

"Billy gave me a hard time. 'What's wrong?' he wanted to know. 'How come we don't get that special table? I like that table—it's nice, it's near a window. A nice view.'

"'I'm sorry, Billy,' I said. 'That table is reserved.'

"'I know it's reserved,' Billy said. 'It's reserved for me and the rest of the team.'

"'Not tonight, Billy,' I said. 'I just can't do it.' And then I made a really big mistake: 'It's reserved for someone really important,' I said.

"You remember Billy Martin, he was never the calmest guy in the world. And when I said that, I thought he was going to start yelling. But all he said, was, 'Oh, yeah? Who's more important than my team after we just won the World Series? Tell me, who?'

"I was doing my best to protect my other guest's privacy, and I was saved from having to say anything by Frank's arrival. When Billy saw Frank coming up the stairs, he got all quiet and his eyes got really big.

"'Hey,' Frank said, when he saw Billy at the top of the stairs, 'what are you doing here?'

"Remember that Frank wasn't always a Yankee fan, but he would have stopped to talk to Billy. Except that Billy was so stunned at seeing Frank face-to-face like that, he couldn't say a word. And Frank went on to his table.

"'Sinatra,' Billy said, 'Frank Sinatra! Wow! He can have my table—he can have the whole Yankee team. Joey, I've always wanted to meet Frank Sinatra. You gotta introduce us. I want to say a real hello to him.'

"'Billy,' I said, 'you saw him, isn't that enough? When Frank comes here, he wants privacy. He likes to eat with his friends, and doesn't want to talk to strangers.'

"'We're not strangers,' Billy shouted, 'we're the New York Yankees, and we just won the World Series.'

"'I know,' I said. 'You're the Yankees, and Frank has always been a Dodger fan.'

"'I'll join the Dodgers,' Billy said, laughing. 'Whatever. You just gotta introduce me to Sinatra.'

"The Yankees settled themselves into a big table up on the second floor, and Frank and his pals got the really private table in the alcove at the back. After they were seated I said to Frank, 'You know, the Yankees are here.'

"'Yeah,' Frank said, laughing, 'and the British are coming.'

"'Frank,' I said, 'Billy Martin wants to come over and say hello. You know—just shake your hand and say hello.'

"'Joey,' Frank said, 'I just flew in from the coast. I don't really feel like glad-handing a bunch of people I don't know.'

"'I know, Frank.' I said, 'And I wouldn't ask you. But this guy Billy Martin—it's so important to him.'

"Frank was quiet for a moment, and then he said, 'Okay, Joey. For you. Bring him over.'

"I left the alcove and walked over to Billy Martin. 'Come on, Billy,' I said, 'I'll introduce you to Frank Sinatra.'

"'Guys,' Billy yelled so loud you could hear him both up- and downstairs in the restaurant. 'Come on. We're going to meet Frank Sinatra!'

"'Billy, I didn't say all forty-eight of you—I thought it was just you.'

"'Come on, Joey, don't keep Frank Sinatra waiting! He wants to meet us.'

"And so the entire Yankee team, lined up behind Billy Martin, followed me as I led the way to Frank's table. You should have seen those guys, they were quiet, polite—they reminded me of kids lined up for confession. I introduced Billy, and he introduced the rest of the team. And Frank shook everyone's hand and congratulated them on their big win.

"After that, the Yankees went back to their table and continued with their party while Frank and his friends had their dinner. Of course, the Yankees didn't want to leave while Frank Sinatra was still there, and it was only after Frank and his party left, waving goodbye, that Billy Martin called me over.

"'Thanks, Joey,' he said, 'you made this an even bigger night for all of us. Now, can I have the check?'

"'No,' I said, 'sorry, Billy, but you can't have the check.'

"'What're you talking about, Joey? What do you mean I can't have the check?'

"'You can't have the check because there is no check,' I told Billy Martin. 'Frank Sinatra paid it.'"

FRANK AND CONCETTA

"Everybody loved my mother," says Anna, "and she worked at the restaurant as hard as my father. When my parents had their first restaurant, on West Forty-ninth Street, the Sorrento, they didn't have a lot of people working for them. Frank Sinatra used to come from the Paramount, and if he saw my mother was busy, he would help out.

"My mother's job was to greet people, answer the phone, take reservations, and make drinks. If Frank was around, and he saw that my mother couldn't get to the phone, he would answer it and take a reservation. And if she was really jammed up, he would get behind the bar and mix drinks.

"After he got divorced from Nancy, he would bring in all the people he went out with—Ava Gardner, Mia Farrow, Juliet Prowse—we met them all. When he became famous, he would use the side entrance and go upstairs to where it's a little more private. I remember one time when I was hosting upstairs, there was a lady standing near me using the telephone. She could see whoever came up the stairs, and I heard her say into the phone, 'I'm not sure, but I think I see Frank Sinatra—I think it is! I think it's Frank Sinatra coming up the stairs!'

"Frank heard her, too, and when he got to the top of the stairs he whispered to her, 'It is.'

"My brother, Joe, bought a bronze statue of Frank when he was in Las Vegas. It looks just like him, the suit, the fedora—just the way he dressed when he sang, 'It's quarter to three, there's no one in the place except you and me.' We have it sitting on the bar right now. Frank was more than a friend to us, he was family. On his birthday, December twelfth, it's our tradition to serve one of his favorite desserts to every guest in the restaurant. We've been doing that for more than twenty years and we still do that, and we also give an annual party in his honor."

THE NIGHT FRANK SINATRA COOKED DINNER FOR BENNETT CERF

"I'm not saying that Frank couldn't cook," says Joe. "He would occasionally go into the kitchen at our restaurant and ask for a taste of a dish, and then suggest adding maybe a little more crushed red pepper or another pinch of oregano. Frank enjoyed food, just as I enjoyed his singing, but he was the singer and I was—and am—the chef.

"Anyway, Frank got a kick out of the idea that people thought of him as a great cook as well as a great singer, and he never bothered to explain that he actually didn't do that much cooking.

"So one time, I don't know exactly how it came about, Frank was invited to Bennett Cerf's house to cook dinner for twelve people. Mr. Cerf was one of the founders and the publisher of Random House, and he knew everybody.

"I get this call from Frank who says, 'Joey, we're going over to Bennett Cerf's house to do a party.' I said fine, and worked out what I was going to cook. The day of the party, I packed up my equipment and the food. Frank sent over a limo and a couple of guys to help carry the stuff, and off we went to Bennett Cerf's house. I arranged everything in the kitchen, and when I heard guests come in, I peeked out—the men were in black tie and the women wore gowns. A lot of distinguished people were there: Frank, of course, Mayor Lindsay and his wife, Mary, Mayor Wagner, people like that. It was when Frank was doing his society thing.

GRANDFATHER PATSY'S *Ledger*

In much the same way that my grandfather started his Wall of Fame, he also had an old-fashioned ledger in which he asked his customers to sign their names. We still have that ledger—and it's a record of show-business royalty.

We keep it in a safe, but I take it out now and then and turn the pages. Grandpa started keeping that ledger in 1946, and luminaries like Mary Pickford, Fred Allen, Joe DiMaggio, and Frances Langford signed its pages.

The names are famous and familiar: Bert Lahr, Al Jolson, Frank Sinatra (he signed in as Frankie, and I guess he was at Patsy's with Tommy Dorsey, whose name is on the following page). Some of the stars mentioned that the food was almost too good—they had to watch their weight then as now—and Marilyn Monroe even drew a stick figure of a girl whose dress was flying up, as hers did in *The Seven Year Itch*.

Rocky Marciano, Deborah Kerr, John Garfield, Guy Lombardo, Vic Damone, Phil Silvers—their names are all there, as are such great singers as Lena Horne and Patti Page. I think my favorite page, though, is the one signed by Sammy Davis Jr. in 1989, shortly before he died. The book had long been put away (my grandfather had used it only until 1954), and one night when my dad was talking about it, Sammy said that he wanted his name in Patsy's ledger, too. So Dad took it out of the vault and Sammy wrote: "It took me fifty-three years, but I finally made it."

"Anyway, after a while, people sat down at the table and Frank came into the kitchen. 'What are we serving first, Joey?' he asked.

"'Clams Posillipo,' I told him. That was one of Frank's favorite dishes. Frank hung out in the kitchen for a little while, just until the clams were done, and then he went back to the dining room. The waiters I had brought with me carried out the clams and served everyone. I opened the door a little and could hear Bennett Cerf say, 'Frank, delicious!' Then everyone applauded.

"That's how it went for the rest of the evening: Frank would come into the kitchen, wait until each dish was ready to be served, and then return to the dining room. I remember there was a Filleto di Pomodoro, followed by Veal Milanese, cooked nice and crisp—the way Frank liked it. Sausages, and meatballs made with veal—again, the way Frank liked them. An arugula salad, zucchini. Each time Frank returned to the dining room, he was greeted with applause. I heard people say, 'Marvelous!' 'Frank, you can do anything!' and 'The best I've ever eaten.' I got a kick out of hearing them rave about Frank's cooking. And when I left quietly by the back door, I could still hear them applauding."

THANKSGIVING FOR FRANK

"We're not open on Thanksgiving Day," says Joe. "My father always figured that was a real family day—people wouldn't want to go to a restaurant. And it gave our family a day off, too.

"But then there was the time we did something different. This was years back— maybe you remember, Frank was having a bad time professionally. He was having trouble with the recording company, and he hadn't yet made *From Here to Eternity*—you know, the movie. And everyone said he was finished.

"We knew he was great, no matter what anyone else said. And whenever Frank came to New York, he would hang out at Patsy's. He was there the day before Thanksgiving having dinner, and you know how terrible people can be? There was Frank Sinatra, and people who knew him just walked right by, didn't talk to him, didn't greet him, nothing. After he finished eating, Frank said to my father, 'I think I'll have Thanksgiving dinner here with you guys. What time are you serving?'

"My dad looked at Frank, and understood how alone he felt. He could have told Frank that the restaurant was closed on Thanksgiving, and invited him home to dinner. But he knew that would hurt Frank's pride, so he just said, 'Three o'clock, Frank. We're serving dinner at three.'

"'Great,' Frank said, 'book me a table.'

"I guess I must have come out of the kitchen at that point, and my father gave me this look and said, 'Frank is having Thanksgiving dinner at the restaurant tomorrow.'

"'Great,' I said, 'what time?'

"'Three o'clock,' my father said. 'You better mark it in the book.'

"I went behind the counter and got out the reservation book and opened it up. Of course, there was nothing written on the page. But Frank couldn't see that, and I wrote his name in and closed the book.

OUR FRIEND *Frank*

What can I say? This man did so much for our family and our business. If you look at our Wall of Fame you can trace almost every celebrity to Frank Sinatra. He brought so many people into Patsy's, and then they brought in other stars, but it all started with Frank. For example, Frank brought in Jackie Gleason, who brought in Tom Hanks. Frank brought in Sammy Davis Jr. and Sammy introduced our restaurant to Debbie Allen, and so on. After Frank died, I read so many tributes to him, and one line was repeated: "He was the best." He certainly was. *Time* said, "You can call him the best, you can call him the greatest, but to call him anything other than Sinatra is to sell him short." We will never forget him, and we're proud and happy to present on the following pages Frank's favorite dishes that he enjoyed eating at his favorite restaurant, Patsy's.

"'So what are you going to make me, Joe?' Frank asked. 'Anything but turkey.'

"'How about a nice Rollatini of Chicken with Spinach Stuffing?' I asked.

"'Sounds great,' Frank said, 'I'll see you guys tomorrow.'

"After Frank left, my father called the staff together and told them that we would be open on Thanksgiving Day. There were some groans and moans. But when my father told them about Sinatra, they understood. And the understanding was helped by my father telling them to bring their families to the restaurant for Thanksgiving dinner.

"And then he got on the phone and called a few friends and invited them, too. One of them was Jerome Castle. Jerry, who was a big wheel on Wall Street and a CEO of a major corporation, said of course he would come.

"'I'd do anything for Patsy,' says Jerome Castle today, remembering that Thanksgiving. 'After all, I'd known him since I was eight years old, when I was taken to the Villanova Restaurant where Patsy worked as a waiter by my father and uncle. And I'd do anything for Frank Sinatra. I knew him from Patsy's—we all hung out there. Yeah, I was there that Thanksgiving. There weren't too many of us.'

"Frank noticed that the restaurant was pretty empty, and he asked my father about it. "'A lot of people stay home on Thanksgiving,' my father said.

"I guess Frank found out about that dinner later on, but he never said anything about it, and neither did we. Once Frank became your friend, he stayed your friend for life. And that's how it was with us."

FRANK SINATRA'S FAVORITES

The following are the recipes for Frank Sinatra's favorite dishes. I don't recommend serving every single dish at the same meal. Frank would often have two servings of the Clams Posillipo, followed by the Veal Milanese—which he wanted prepared extra-crisp. Other times he might have the Arugula Salad followed by the Fusilli with Garlic and Anchovies.

You'll notice as you read these recipes that garlic was handled in a special way for Frank. He enjoyed the flavor of garlic as long as it was used with a light touch and was not visible in the completed dish. That's why when we cooked for him, we would cut garlic cloves in half, sauté them very lightly in oil, and then discard them before continuing with the recipe, using the flavored oil but not the cloves. In some dishes, such as the Arugula Salad, we would omit the garlic entirely.

Frank loved our desserts, and the Lemon Ricotta Torte (page 210) was a favorite. If you're planning to serve Pasticiotto or Sfogliatelle, I recommend a visit to a good Italian pastry shop. Or come to Patsy's, where these pastries are prepared in our restaurant. That's what Frank did.

Frank's Clams Posillipo

SERVES 4

32 littleneck clams
3 tablespoons olive oil
6 garlic cloves, halved
1 small yellow onion, chopped (about
¼ cup)
1 28-ounce can whole plum tomatoes,
with juice

Salt and freshly ground black pepper, to
taste
1 tablespoon tomato paste (optional)
¼ cup chopped fresh basil
1 tablespoon chopped fresh flat-leaf
parsley, plus more for garnish

Scrub the clamshells, rinse thoroughly in cold water, and place in a large pot. Add cold water to cover and bring to a boil over high heat. Cook until the shells open, about 5 minutes. Using a slotted spoon, transfer the clams to a large bowl. Discard any clams that have not opened.

Strain the cooking liquid through a chinois or a strainer lined with a coffee filter, and reserve ¾ cup of this liquid as clam broth. Return the clams to the pot, add cold water, and stir to remove any remaining sand. Drain and reserve.

Heat the oil in a large saucepan over medium flame and sauté the garlic halves until golden, about 2 minutes. With a slotted spoon or tongs, remove and discard the garlic. Add the onions to the saucepan and sauté for 3 to 4 minutes, until soft and translucent. Coarsely chop the tomatoes and add with their juice to the saucepan and bring to a boil. Reduce the heat to low, cover, and simmer for 25 minutes, stirring occasionally.

Season to taste with salt and pepper. Stir in the tomato paste (if using) and add the basil and parsley. Simmer uncovered for 5 minutes.

Add the reserved clam broth and clams to the sauce and bring to a boil. Cover, reduce the heat to low, and simmer for 8 to 10 minutes, or until the clams are heated through. Spoon the clams and sauce into a large serving bowl, garnish with parsley, and serve immediately.

Frank's Stuffed Artichokes

SERVES 4

4 large or jumbo artichokes

2 garlic cloves, halved

1 cup dry bread crumbs

2 tablespoons finely chopped black olives, preferably gaeta

2 tablespoons freshly grated Parmigiano-Reggiano

1 tablespoon chopped fresh flat-leaf parsley

1 tablespoon chopped fresh basil

1 tablespoon chopped nonpareil capers, rinsed and drained

¼ teaspoon crushed red pepper flakes

¼ teaspoon dried oregano

¼ teaspoon freshly ground black pepper, plus more to taste

3 tablespoons olive oil

Salt, to taste

Preheat the oven to 450°F.

Rinse the artichokes under cold running water. With a sharp knife, remove the stem, and cut 2 inches from the top of each artichoke. Pull the center leaves apart, and with a small spoon remove the fuzzy choke and tiny inner leaves. Insert a garlic half into the hollowed-out artichoke center. Reserve.

Place the bread crumbs, olives, cheese, parsley, basil, capers, red pepper flakes, oregano, and ¼ teaspoon pepper in a large mixing bowl. Add the olive oil gradually, stirring until thoroughly combined and moistened. Spoon the bread-crumb mixture into the hollowed-out artichoke centers, tamping down with the back of a spoon until each artichoke is filled to the top. Season to taste with salt and additional pepper.

Place the artichokes in a baking dish and add enough water to cover the bottom halves of the artichokes. Cover the pan with foil, and bake in the preheated oven for 1 hour and 15 minutes, until the artichokes are cooked through. Check for tenderness by removing a leaf or two after 1 hour and tasting. If the water level drops to less than ½ inch while cooking, add more.

Remove from the oven and increase the heat to broil. Take off the foil and place the artichokes under the broiler until the bread-crumb topping has browned, about 2 to 3 minutes.

Place the artichokes on a serving platter and spoon 2 to 4 tablespoons of the pan juices over each artichoke. Garlic may be omitted, if desired, as Frank did.

Frank's Arugula Salad

SERVES 4

2 bunches arugula, trimmed
⅓ cup olive oil
3 tablespoons red wine vinegar

1 tablespoon finely chopped fresh basil
  (about 4 leaves)
Salt and freshly ground black pepper,
  to taste

Swish the arugula in a large bowl of cold water to remove the sand and grit. Allow it to soak, then drain, rinse, and repeat the procedure with clean water until the water remains clear. Dry the leaves, and tear into bite-size pieces.

Combine the oil, vinegar, and chopped basil in a screw-top jar. Close tightly and shake until thoroughly blended. Toss the arugula with the dressing in a large bowl, and arrange on four plates. Season with salt and pepper.

Frank's Fusilli with Garlic and Anchovies

SERVES 4

¼ cup olive oil
6 garlic cloves, quartered
1 small yellow onion, chopped (about
  ¼ cup)
10 anchovies, chopped
Salt and freshly ground black pepper, to
  taste

½ cup chopped fresh basil
1 tablespoon chopped fresh flat-leaf
  parsley
1 pound fusilli, cooked al dente
4 tablespoons Seasoned Bread Crumbs
  (page 49)

Heat the oil in a large saucepan over medium flame and sauté the garlic until golden, about 2 minutes. With a slotted spoon or tongs, remove and discard the garlic. Add the onions to the saucepan and sauté for 3 to 4 minutes, until soft and translucent. Add the anchovies and 1⅓ cups water. Bring to a boil, reduce the heat to low, cover, and simmer for 4 minutes, stirring occasionally. Season to taste with salt and pepper. Add the basil and parsley. Simmer uncovered for 2 minutes, and remove from the heat.

Heat a nonstick skillet over medium-high flame, add the bread crumbs, and toss gently until lightly browned.

Place the cooked fusilli in a large serving bowl. Spoon the sauce over the pasta and toss to combine. Sprinkle with the toasted bread crumbs and serve immediately.

Frank's Veal Cutlets Milanese

SERVES 8

½ small Italian stale baguette (about ½ pound)

2 tablespoons freshly grated Parmigiano-Reggiano

Pinch of oregano

¼ cup minced flat-leaf parsley

1 cup plus 3 tablespoons olive oil

¼ teaspoon salt

⅛ teaspoon freshly ground black pepper

½ cup all-purpose flour

2 large eggs, beaten

8 veal cutlets (about 1¼ pounds), pounded thin to slightly less than ¼ inch

Salt and freshly ground black pepper, to taste

1 lemon, cut into 8 wedges

Break or cut the bread into large chunks and place in a food processor. Process until the bread is reduced to fine crumbs. Transfer the crumbs to a large bowl and stir in the cheese, oregano, and parsley. Gradually add 3 tablespoons of oil, stirring, until thoroughly combined. Season with the salt and pepper.

Spread the flour on a large plate, place the eggs in a shallow bowl, and spread the seasoned bread crumbs on a second large plate. Coat each veal cutlet in the flour, then the beaten eggs, and then the bread crumbs, patting with the palm of your hand to ensure adhesion.

Heat 1 cup of the oil in a large nonstick skillet over medium-high flame (to a frying temperature of 350°F.) and sauté the veal for 2 minutes. Turn and sauté for 1 additional minute. Do not crowd the pan. If necessary, fry the cutlets in batches. Remove with a slotted spatula and drain on paper towels. Season to taste with salt and pepper, and serve with lemon wedges.

WE HAVE SOME GREAT APPETIZERS ON OUR MENU, FAMILIAR dishes that everyone loves, like Mussels Arreganata and an assortment of antipasti, both hot and cold. But we let our guests choose from every section of the menu when it comes to the way they want to start their meals. Some want a salad, while others want spicy sausages made with hot cherry peppers; the choice is theirs. When you're planning a dinner, you should give yourself plenty of leeway, too. You could serve something light like Figs with Mascarpone and Prosciutto, or you might go with a heartier starter, such as a slice of Timballo—a small slice, because you want your guests to go on to the next course. So when you're looking for first-course suggestions, try leafing through the entire book: You might find ideas in the chapters on salads or main courses.

APPETIZERS

STUFFED ARTICHOKES

ASPARAGUS ROLLS

JOE'S EGGPLANT SANDWICH

FIGS WITH PROSCIUTTO AND MASCARPONE

ROASTED PORTOBELLO MUSHROOMS
    AND ASPARAGUS

PORTOBELLO TOWER

SEASONED BREAD CRUMBS

MUSSELS ARREGANATA

ROASTED RED BELL PEPPERS

PEPPERS SICILIANO

PALLE DI RISO (RICE BALLS)

SHRIMP WITH SAUTÉED FENNEL
    OVER MESCLUN SALAD

TOMATO BRUSCHETTA

VEGETABLE NAPOLEON

STUFFED
ARTICHOKES

ONE OF FRANK SINATRA'S VERY FAVORITE RECIPES. BELOW IS OUR TYPICAL preparation, but we changed it slightly to accommodate Frank's aversion to a strong garlic taste (see page 31).

SERVES 4

4 large or jumbo artichokes

1 cup dry bread crumbs

2 tablespoons finely chopped black
   olives, preferably gaeta

2 tablespoons grated Parmigiano-
   Reggiano

1 garlic clove, pressed or minced

1 tablespoon chopped fresh flat-leaf
   parsley

1 tablespoon chopped fresh basil

1 tablespoon chopped nonpareil capers,
   rinsed and drained

¼ teaspoon crushed red pepper flakes

¼ teaspoon dried oregano

¼ teaspoon freshly ground black pepper,
   plus more to taste

3 tablespoons olive oil

Salt, to taste

Preheat the oven to 450°F.

Rinse the artichokes under cold running water. With a sharp knife, remove the stem, and cut 2 inches from the top of each artichoke. Pull the center leaves apart, and with a small spoon remove the fuzzy choke and tiny inner leaves. Reserve.

Place the bread crumbs, olives, cheese, garlic, parsley, basil, capers, red pepper flakes, oregano, and ¼ teaspoon pepper in a large mixing bowl. Add the olive oil gradually, stirring until thoroughly combined and moistened. Spoon the bread-crumb mixture into the hollowed-out artichoke centers, tamping down with the back of the spoon until each artichoke is filled to the top. Season to taste with salt and additional pepper.

Place the artichokes in a baking dish and add enough water to cover the bottom halves of the artichokes. Cover the pan with foil, and bake in the preheated oven for 1 hour and 15 minutes, until artichokes are cooked through. Check for tenderness by removing a leaf or two after 1 hour and tasting. If the water level drops to less than $\frac{1}{2}$ inch while cooking, add more.

Remove from the oven and increase the heat to broil. Take off the foil and place the artichokes under the broiler until the bread-crumb topping has browned, about 2 to 3 minutes.

Place the artichokes on a serving platter and spoon 2 to 4 tablespoons of the pan juices over each artichoke.

Nick Clooney

"Work and family have brought me to New York City regularly since I was a teenager," says Nick Clooney, newspaper columnist and host of radio and television programs. "Patsy's Restaurant on West Fifty-sixth Street and Eighth Avenue has always been a part of that New York experience.

"My first meals at Patsy's were in 1949 when I was fifteen. Even then, Patsy's had long been the talk of the town. I well remember how my ears perked up when 'my' Patsy's was mentioned on the popular Barry Gray radio program on WMCA in New York. Barry was interviewing Frank Sinatra and asked him if he was going to Patsy's the next night for dinner. Mr. Sinatra said, no, he planned to go to another restaurant.

"As it happened, my sister Rosemary and I went to Patsy's the next night and there was Frank—whom I had never seen in person before—along with a group of his friends. He came over to say hello to Rosemary, who then introduced me. I was brash enough to say I had heard the radio show and what was he doing at Patsy's? He said, 'I tell everybody I'm going to that other restaurant so they don't bug me when I come to Patsy's. I always come to Patsy's.'

"He was not alone. I have dined at Patsy's often in each of the intervening years since 1949, always with a cross-section of people that invariably included a sprinkling of famous faces.

"I was happy to bring my wife to Patsy's not long after we were married, and our children, Ada and George, have found Patsy's part of their lives as well. We have hosted a number of celebrations there, including a birthday dinner for George a few years ago. In the twelve years I have written my column for the *Cincinnati Post*, Patsy's has twice had full pieces devoted to their food, service, and memories.

"Clearly, Patsy's—including the entire Scognamillo family, their colleagues, and friends—has been a consistent and rich strand running through our New York experience. It will remain so."

ASPARAGUS ROLLS

THERE ARE MANY WAYS TO COOK ASPARAGUS, BUT I FIND THE FOLLOWING method easiest. Break off the bottom inch of each asparagus stalk and discard. Rinse the asparagus and place in one layer in a large skillet. Add water almost to cover. Bring to a boil, then lower the heat to a simmer, cover, and cook until just tender. Depending on the age and thickness of the asparagus, that could be anywhere from 5 to 10 minutes. Check tenderness frequently with a fork.

SERVES 4

2 tablespoons ricotta

3 tablespoons finely chopped mozzarella

6 tablespoons grated Parmigiano-
   Reggiano

4 paper-thin slices prosciutto (each
   approximately 3 inches by 6 inches)

1 pound thin asparagus (about 16 to 20
   spears), cooked (see headnote) and
   chilled

¼ teaspoon salt

¼ teaspoon freshly ground black pepper

¼ cup olive oil

6 garlic cloves, finely chopped

2½ cups chopped fresh plum tomatoes

2 tablespoons finely chopped fresh basil

2 tablespoons finely chopped fresh
   flat-leaf parsley

⅓ cup dry white wine

Preheat the broiler.

In a small mixing bowl, combine the ricotta, mozzarella, and 4 tablespoons of the Parmigiano-Reggiano and mix thoroughly. Reserve.

Place a slice of prosciutto on a cutting board. Divide the cooked asparagus evenly into 4 portions. Line up 1 portion (about 4 to 5 spears) on the prosciutto slice. Top with a quarter of the cheese mixture. Season with salt and pepper. Fold the ends of the prosciutto over the asparagus, and roll until the asparagus and cheese is completely wrapped in prosciutto. Repeat for the remaining 3 portions.

Heat the olive oil in a large nonstick skillet over medium flame. Place the asparagus rolls cheese side up in the skillet and sauté for 2 to 3 minutes, or until the cheese begins to melt. Remove from the skillet and place in a shallow nonstick baking pan. Set aside.

Add the garlic to the skillet and sauté over medium heat until golden, about 1 to 2 minutes. Add the chopped tomatoes, basil, parsley, and wine. Bring to a boil, then reduce heat to a simmer, cover, and cook for 5 to 6 minutes, or until the ingredients are blended and heated through.

Sprinkle the asparagus rolls with the remaining 2 tablespoons of grated Parmigiano-Reggiano. Place in the broiler and cook until the cheese has melted and is lightly browned, about 2 to 3 minutes.

Spoon 2 to 3 tablespoons of sauce in the center of 4 plates. Place an asparagus roll on top of the sauce, and garnish with additional sauce.

MAKING DO

"When I was growing up," says Joe, "we had to learn how to make do with very little. My mother could make a wonderful meal out of potatoes, pieces of broken macaroni, onions, garlic, and any other vegetables we had in the house, all cooked together with some olive oil and water.

"When we had tomatoes, we had a feast. My mother would slice the tomatoes nice and thin, and season them with salt, pepper, and garlic, and spoon olive oil over them. We would dunk our bread in that tomato-flavored oil and then eat the tomatoes. Today, all kinds of antipasto are made with tomatoes and oil. Bruschetta, for instance, that's considered gourmet and high cuisine. Years ago, that was a poor man's food. My mother just thought of it as a delicious and cheap way to feed her family."

Joe Scognamillo
THE MAKING OF A CHEF

I was six or seven when I started working in a pastry shop in Little Italy. I remember it was on the corner of Kenmare and Mott streets. My job was to scrub pots and pans after the bakers left, and I did my best to please my boss—I even obeyed him when he told me that he wanted me to whistle while I worked. I didn't understand the sense of that until one of the bakers said, "Stupid kid, the boss knows that if you're whistling your mouth is empty so you can't be eating the cakes."

I had a lot of different jobs as a kid—I shined shoes and racked up balls in a billiard parlor. My boss at the bakery said he was doing me a favor, teaching me the business and making me an apprentice baker.

Those were hard times, and even as a little kid I understood that. My father had landed on Ellis Island after first going to Cuba from Naples, and he took whatever jobs he could get. He worked as a waiter at the Westchester Country Club, drove a truck for Macy's, and went back to the restaurant business as a waiter at the Grotto Azzurro in Little Italy.

In those days there were only two important Italian restaurants in New York—one was the Grotto Azzurro and the other was the Red Devil. A bookmaker named Joe, also known as Downtown Joe, came along and told my father that he wanted him to open another Italian restaurant. That's how the Villanova came into being. My father named the Villanova after a town in Naples, and he launched the restaurant: He hired the help, created the menu, bought the supplies—did everything. The restaurant did so well that my father was able to expand the operation for Joe by taking over a store next door, then two adjacent stores. That's where my father first became friendly with celebrities as diverse as Enrico Caruso and Lucky Luciano.

You got to understand those times: Downtown Joe was not a nice guy. My father did all the work and he took all the money. Some nights my mother and I went down to meet my father, but we weren't allowed to wait in the restaurant—he didn't even want us on the same side of the street. When I said to my mother that I just wanted to look into the Villanova—see where my father worked—my mother said I couldn't. Joe would get mad. So we waited across the street, and on cold nights we would go into the old Gaiety Delicatessen and my mother would order a cup of coffee, nothing else, while we waited for my father to get through with work.

After a while, my father and a partner opened the Sorrento. That was great—our own place! Now I was allowed to be in the restaurant, and I was even given a job—I filled the salt and pepper shakers. I guess I was about nine or ten by then. My salary? A stick of gum. A few years later, I went to work in the kitchen, and I learned to cook the way chefs do in Europe—from the ground up. I peeled potatoes, cleaned shrimp, strained sauces, chopped garlic.

The Sorrento was on West Forty-ninth Street, and it was a favorite hangout for all the well-known musicians and singers working nearby. That's when we first met Frank Sinatra —he would come in looking real sharp in his camelhair coat. Tommy Dorsey. People like that. When other guests in the restaurant saw Frank come in, they would run to the jukebox and put in money to play Frank's records. It was flattering, but Frank hated it. He didn't want to be serenaded by his own records, though it was a well-meant gesture. My father understood him, and when he saw Frank come in he would disconnect the jukebox.

The Sorrento was doing well, but my father and his partner began to have disagreements, and my father decided it was time to move on. He left the Sorrento, and came up to Fifty-sixth Street and opened up Patsy's. It turned out to be a blessing in disguise, because by that time I was around seventeen, and I knew enough to take over the kitchen. I was a full-time chef and proud to be one.

I now work mostly in the dining room, but my favorite job is behind the stove.

JOE'S
EGGPLANT SANDWICH

"THIS WAS ONE OF MY MOTHER'S WONDERFUL INVENTIONS AT A TIME WHEN she had a large family and very little money," says Joe. "One big eggplant could go far, as she and other Neapolitans knew. Eggplant could be used as a main course—that's where Eggplant Parmigiana comes from. And it added body and flavor to soups, sauces, and stews.

"When we were kids, we looked forward to eating what we called an Eggplant Sandwich when we came home from school. My mother called it Torta di Melanzane, an eggplant cake. 'Speak English,' we would beg her, 'speak English'—the cry of many children of immigrant parents. Today I love the joke of it—an eggplant sandwich, an unpretentious name for a delicious dish. I've been in the restaurant business long enough to have gotten past the need to give every dish a 'continental' name on a menu. So here's my recipe for an early favorite. Serve it as an appetizer; it goes especially well with a Campari-and-soda or a dry Pinot Grigio; Santa Margherita is my favorite."

SERVES 10

1 large eggplant (about 1¼ pounds)

½ cup all-purpose flour

5 eggs, lightly beaten

1 cup olive oil, plus more for deep-frying

½ teaspoon salt

¼ teaspoon freshly ground black pepper

2 Roasted Red Bell Peppers (page 52), each sliced into 5 pieces

10 thin slices (about ½ pound) mozzarella

10 thin slices (about ¼ pound) prosciutto

10 large basil leaves

3 to 4 cups grated Parmigiano-Reggiano

Trim the ends of the eggplant and peel. Cut it lengthwise into 10 slices, approximately ¼ inch or less in thickness.

Spread the flour on a large plate. Coat each eggplant slice in the flour, and then dip in the beaten egg. Reserve the leftover egg.

Heat the oil in a large nonstick skillet over medium-high flame. Add the battered eggplant slices in batches (don't crowd the pan) and sauté for about 5 minutes, or until lightly browned on both sides. Remove with a slotted spatula and drain on paper towels. Season with salt and pepper and allow to cool.

When the eggplant is cool enough to handle, assemble the sandwiches. Line up the 10 eggplant slices on a work surface. Place a slice of roasted pepper on half of each slice, and top with a slice each of mozzarella and prosciutto and a leaf of basil. Fold the other half of each slice up and over the ingredients, creating a sandwich. Spread the Parmigiano-Reggiano on a large plate. Coat each sandwich with the remainder of the beaten egg, and roll it in the plate of grated cheese. Wrap the sandwiches in plastic wrap and refrigerate for 1 to 2 hours, or until thoroughly chilled and firm.

Heat 2 inches of oil in a deep skillet to a frying temperature of 375°F. Fry the sandwiches one at a time, turning carefully until the cheese crust is golden and crisp, about 3 to 4 minutes. Drain on paper towels and serve immediately.

HOMEMADE *Vinegar*

"We never threw anything out," says Joe. "My mother would make vinegar out of leftover wine. She would transfer the wine to a large jar, add a few pieces of pasta, which would cause the wine to ferment, and let it sit for two or three weeks. After that she would strain out the pasta and we had the real thing—wine vinegar. We don't do this anymore and you shouldn't try it at home."

FIGS WITH PROSCIUTTO AND MASCARPONE

I THINK MASCARPONE WORKS BEST IN THIS RECIPE, BUT OTHER SOFT CHEESES such as the French Saint André or Explorateur will also do.

SERVES 4

8 large fresh figs, green or black

4 tablespoons mascarpone cheese, at room temperature

8 thin slices (about ¼ pound) good-quality prosciutto, each slice cut in half lengthwise

4 small servings Mesclun Salad wih Vinaigrette (page 71)

Wash figs gently under cold running water. Cut each fig in half lengthwise.

Using a butter knife, spread equal amounts of mascarpone on the prosciutto slices. Wrap each fig half in a slice of prosciutto.

Divide the salad among 4 plates, and top each serving with 4 fig halves.

"*Eating at Patsy's is like swinging with Frank Sinatra!*" —MAURICE HINES

Friselle
OR FAZELLE (HOWEVER YOU SPELL IT, IT'S DELICIOUS!)

"Friselle are a wonderful snack," says Joe. "They're made with leftover bread—maybe a ciabatta or a pane rustica, whatever you have in the house.

"When we were kids, my mother would make Friselle and then break them up and add them to bowls of soup. Today they're served as a snack—they're great with an aperitivo, and you can serve them with chunks of really good Parmigiano-Reggiano or provolone and a few slices of soppressata salami. Today you can buy Friselle at most good Italian bakeries, but you can also make them at home from leftover Italian bread.

"You slice the bread, not too thin, and toast it in a 300 degree oven until it's really dry, maybe 5 or 10 minutes, but you don't want the bread to get too hard. Next you moisten it with a little water. Then you combine olive oil, balsamic vinegar, some chopped tomato, fresh basil, one or two crushed garlic cloves, and a pinch of oregano. Mix it all up and spoon it over the bread. Season it with a little salt and pepper. You can serve the Friselle right away, or they'll keep for a few days in the refrigerator in an airtight container. Everyone loves them."

ROASTED
PORTOBELLO MUSHROOMS
AND ASPARAGUS

NOT TOO LONG AGO, PORTOBELLO MUSHROOMS WERE EXTREMELY expensive, but today—thanks to the California growers—Portobellos are available in many supermarkets, and affordable. I don't recommend substituting mushrooms such as porcini, chanterelles, or morels—they're far too expensive, and I find that the wonderful, meaty Portobellos work better than the more delicate mushrooms.

SERVES 4 TO 6

¼ cup olive oil, plus more for coating pan

4 medium Portobello mushroom caps (about ¼ pound), rinsed and patted dry

½ teaspoon salt

¼ teaspoon freshly ground pepper

¾ pound asparagus (about 16 spears), washed and trimmed

8 garlic cloves, thinly sliced

6 tablespoons balsamic vinegar

¼ cup minced fresh basil

¼ cup minced fresh flat-leaf parsley

½ cup chicken broth

Preheat the oven to 400°F.

Coat a baking pan with a small amount of the olive oil. Place the mushrooms cap side down in the pan, season with salt and pepper, and roast for 12 minutes, or until just tender. Allow the mushrooms to cool, then slice thin.

Meanwhile, place the asparagus in one layer in a large skillet. Add water to cover and cook over low heat until just tender, 5 to 10 minutes. Drain and set aside.

Heat the remaining ¼ cup of oil in a saucepan over medium flame. Add the garlic and sauté, stirring, for 2 minutes, or until lightly browned. Add the cooked mushrooms and asparagus, and the vinegar, basil, and parsley, and cook an additional minute. Add the chicken broth and stir to combine. Cover the saucepan and simmer for 2 to 3 minutes, or until all ingredients are blended and heated through.

Remove the vegetables with a spatula and place on a serving platter. Spoon the sauce over the vegetables and serve.

PORTOBELLO TOWER

THE LOOK OF A DISH DEFINITELY AFFECTS THE APPETITE. AND THIS TOWER has enchanted many of our customers—as it will guests at your next dinner party. It can be served over greens or on its own for a spectacular first course, or as a side dish.

SERVES 4

4 large Portobello mushroom caps

½ cup olive oil, plus more for coating pan

Salt and freshly ground black pepper, to taste

1 large zucchini (about ½ pound), sliced ¼ inch thick

2 small Italian eggplants (about ½ pound total)

¼ pound provolone, thinly sliced

1 Roasted Red Bell Pepper (page 52), quartered

¼ pound mozzarella, thinly sliced

Preheat the oven to 450°F. Rinse the mushrooms and pat dry.

Lightly coat a 13 × 9 × 2-inch baking pan with olive oil. Place the mushrooms, cap side down, in the pan and bake for 10 to 14 minutes, or until the mushrooms are tender. Sprinkle with salt and pepper and reserve. Don't turn off the oven or clean the pan.

Heat 1 to 2 tablespoons of olive oil in a large nonstick skillet over medium flame. Add the zucchini slices and sauté, turning once, until lightly browned, about 5 minutes. Remove with a slotted spoon, sprinkle with salt and pepper, and reserve.

Remove the stems from the eggplants, halve each lengthwise, then cut into ¼-inch crescent slices. Adding more oil if necessary and keeping the skillet hot at all times, add the eggplant and sauté, turning once, until lightly browned on both sides, about 5 minutes. Remove with a slotted spoon, sprinkle with salt and pepper, and reserve.

Re-oil the baking dish, if necessary, and add the mushrooms cap side down. Create layers by topping each mushroom with the zucchini, eggplant, provolone, red pepper, and mozzarella on top. Bake for 6 to 8 minutes, or until the cheese has melted and ingredients are heated through. Allow to rest for 5 minutes before serving.

Rush Limbaugh

"Shortly after arriving in New York in 1988, I became aware of Patsy's. I read about the place and heard people talk about it, but I didn't go. Why? Well, the place was spoken about with such reverence that I thought it was the kind of place you had to 'earn' admission to. It seemed that only famous celebrities went there. Why, this was Frank Sinatra's hangout when he was in town. How in the world could I get in there?

"So for two years I continued to read about all the fun that was going on at Patsy's, but I honestly didn't have the courage to pop in. I got so intrigued by the seeming mystery of the place that I began discussing it on my radio show, treating it as a forbidden place, openly wondering what would happen if I tried to get in. Roger Ailes, now the president of Fox News Channel, eventually told me I should just go and took me. And I will never forget the moment we arrived. Joey Scognamillo, who I had never met, beamed at me, walked up eagerly, and said, *"Mega Dittos!"* I honestly couldn't believe it. That he would know or care. Now, I know this must all sound a bit strange and naive, but I had never been to New York before and had certain perceptions of the city that were mistaken. I thought New York was a place you had to prove yourself in every way, including entry to the city's finest restaurants. But I was wrong, and especially about Patsy's.

"Patsy's became my home for dinner, for all intents and purposes. I have never felt more welcome or comfortable anywhere. They prepare whatever I want, whether it is on the menu or not, exactly as I specify. And they don't do that just for me; they try to do that for everyone. During the four years of my TV show, literally half the studio audience (sometimes more) would trek over for dinner each night after our taping. During special occasions, Joey, Frank, and Sal would cater big spreads in the studio. And I recall one night throwing fried calamari into the studio audience during a show in which I was teasing Mary Tyler Moore about adopting and saving some old lobster named Larry, who was housed in a tank in a restaurant on the Left Coast. People left their seats chasing the stuff.

"Whenever I wanted privacy, they would close half the top floor and actually give me the Sinatra Room to do whatever I needed to do, be it business or pleasure.

"But if you want to know about the people who are Patsy's, try this. The first Thanksgiving dinner my wife, Marta (who, by the way, I proposed to at Patsy's, and she accepted), and I spent in New York was actually prepared by Sal, the Big Honcho Chef at Patsy's. He showed up Thanksgiving morning and opened Patsy's kitchen (the restaurant was closed all day), and prepared a complete Thanksgiving dinner for my family, to my specifications. And the whole thing was their idea. All I had to do was arrange to have it picked up. Sal gave up his Thanksgiving morning with his family to do this for us. I will never forget it. The thing is that every time I visit Patsy's I am made to feel as a member of the Patsy's family, which I suppose I am. And you will be, too. All you have to do is go that first time. They will never forget you and you won't forget them. You will go back and back and back. And when you're there, take a quick look around. You never know who you might see dining right next to you."

SEASONED
BREAD CRUMBS

YOU CAN BUY PACKAGED SEASONED BREAD CRUMBS, AND IF YOU'RE IN a hurry it's okay to do that. But to get a really flavorful bread-crumb mixture, I recommend making it at home. It's not hard. You can grate the bread in a food processor and then stir in the other ingredients. It's also a great way to use yesterday's leftover bread. No leftover bread? Okay: Buy a package of plain bread crumbs and season with the ingredients below.

MAKES ABOUT 1 CUP

½ small Italian stale baguette (about ½ pound)

2 tablespoons freshly grated Parmigiano-Reggiano

¼ cup minced flat-leaf parsley

Pinch of oregano

1 garlic clove, minced

3 tablespoons olive oil

Salt and freshly ground black pepper, to taste

Break or cut the bread into large chunks and place in a food processor. Process until reduced to fine crumbs. Transfer the crumbs to a large bowl. Stir in the cheese, parsley, oregano, and garlic. Gradually add oil, stirring, until thoroughly combined. Season to taste with salt and pepper.

Place in an airtight jar, cover, and refrigerate until needed. Use within 5 days.

Anne Meara
AND THE WHITE-TABLECLOTH RESTAURANT

"I equate Patsy's with our first white-tablecloth restaurant, the first one we could afford to go to," says Anne. "It was after Jerry and I appeared on the *Ed Sullivan Show*, and we went to Patsy's to celebrate. It's still the restaurant of choice for the whole family. We went there with our children, Amy and Ben Stiller, to celebrate the opening of one of Ben's films.

"Patsy's really has the feeling of an Old World restaurant. They're gracious. If you want something and it isn't on the menu, Joe or Sal will say, 'We'll make it for you.' We used to go there a lot with Nancy and Carroll O'Connor; they loved it, too. Carroll said that Patsy's Sauce Puttanesca was better than the same sauce he had in Rome when he lived in Italy.

"What do I like to eat at Patsy's? The Roasted Peppers with Anchovies and Capers, the Arugula Salad, the Clams or Mussels Arreganata, and the Capellini with Marinara Sauce."

MUSSELS ARREGANATA

WE PREPARE ARREGANATA RECIPES WITH LOBSTERS AS WELL AS MUSSELS, but I think this slightly less familiar dish makes an interesting change from an old favorite.

To clean mussels, use a small knife to scrape the barnacles from the shells and to cut off the beard-like strands. Place the mussels in a large pot, cover with cold water, and soak for 10 minutes. Drain and repeat several times with fresh water until the water is clear.

SERVES 4

24 mussels, washed and cleaned (see above)

¼ teaspoon freshly ground black pepper

1 cup Seasoned Bread Crumbs (page 49)

¼ cup olive oil

2 lemons, each cut into wedges

Preheat the broiler.

Place the mussels in a large saucepan and add cold water to cover. Bring to a boil and cook over high heat for 10 minutes, or until mussels open. Discard those that have not opened.

Transfer the mussels to a colander and rinse under cold water until they are cool enough to handle. Shuck the mussels, discard half the shells, and place the mussel meat in the remaining half shells. Season with pepper.

Spoon the bread crumbs on the mussels and smooth with the back of a spoon. Arrange the mussels in one layer in a broiler pan, and drizzle lightly with the olive oil to moisten.

Broil until the bread crumbs are lightly browned, about 2 to 3 minutes. Remove and serve hot with lemon wedges.

ROASTED
RED BELL PEPPERS

ROASTED RED BELL PEPPERS ARE ONE OF THE MOST VERSATILE INGREDIENTS in my kitchen, and I think you'll find many uses for them in yours. They can be enjoyed with nothing more than a splash of oil and vinegar, or they can be combined with anchovies, olives, and garlic, or used as a colorful garnish over broiled fish or meat.

MAKES 4 PEPPERS

4 red bell peppers, rinsed

Preheat the broiler.

Line a broiling pan with aluminum foil. Place the peppers in the pan and broil for 15 to 20 minutes, turning frequently, until peppers are charred black on all sides.

Remove the peppers from the pan and place in a paper bag. Allow to cool for about 10 minutes. When cool enough to handle, hold each pepper under cold, running water and scrape away the charred skin using a paring knife. Rinse the peppers to remove the last bits of skin, and place on paper towels to dry.

The peppers may now be sliced and served with olive oil and pressed garlic as an appetizer or side dish, or used as an ingredient in other recipes.

THERE'S A LOT TO OUR NAME

We're proud of our name, Patsy's Italian Restaurant, after Patsy Scognamillo, my grandfather. You will find us at one and only one location: 236 West Fifth-sixth Street. Our restaurant is the product of three generations: my grandfather; my dad, Joe, and my aunt, Anna, who have been working in Patsy's since they were kids; my mother, Rose; and then there's my cousin Frank and me. You may meet one or all of us when you come to the restaurant. My father or Frank will greet you at the door and take you to a table. Later on, one of them is sure to stop by and make sure that everything you've ordered is the way you like it. When you leave, my mother or aunt will be at the register, and they'll say goodbye, and ask if everything was okay. If you don't see me, that's because I'm in the kitchen, but I often run out in my chef's whites to make sure everything is going right.

Years ago, when Frank Sinatra had a home in Palm Springs, he asked my grandfather to open a branch there. "Can't do it," my grandfather told him. "To be good we have to be at one restaurant, we have to watch every little thing, and we can't do that in two places." Frank understood.

IT'S
Dinah Shore CALLING

"A lot of our customers call us at home," says Joe, "usually on a day when the restaurant isn't open—not that there are too many days like that. Or they're in show business and live in California—that's where most of our calls come from—and they want to make a dish they've eaten at Patsy's, and they don't know how.

"One of my favorite calls came at home one Sunday when I was off. The phone rang and my wife, Rose, answered it. I was reading the paper, but I looked up when the phone rang and I could see Rose looking a little puzzled—maybe even annoyed. She put the receiver down without hang-ing up and said to me, 'It's for you. She says she's Dinah Shore.'

"I got up and went to the phone and said hello. 'Joe,' I heard a familiar voice with a slight Southern accent, 'Joe, I'm really sorry to bother you on a Sunday, but I'm having some people to lunch. You think you could give me the recipe for Peppers Siciliano over the phone? I'd sure appreciate it.'

"'Sure, Dinah,' I said. 'Got paper and pencil?' And I proceeded to give Dinah Shore the recipe for her favorite Patsy's dish—Peppers Siciliano.

"'Rose,' I said, after I hung up, 'that really was Dinah Shore.'"

PEPPERS SICILIANO

HERE'S THE SOUTHERN ITALIAN WAY OF PRESENTING ROASTED PEPPERS, with garlic, capers, anchovies, and olives creating a piquant dish. Please don't be afraid of anchovies. Not many people appreciate these tiny, flavorful fish. Buy them packed in oil with salt, and do not drain or rinse. When I'm working with anchovies I usually eat one or two without adding anything to them.

SERVES 4 TO 6

¼ cup olive oil, plus 2 tablespoons for drizzling

4 garlic cloves, minced

4 Roasted Red Bell Peppers (page 52), each sliced into 4 to 6 pieces

1 tablespoon chopped anchovies with oil

2 tablespoons nonpareil capers, rinsed and drained

3 tablespoons pitted, chopped gaeta or kalamata olives (about 18 olives)

2 tablespoons chopped fresh basil

Pinch of oregano

⅓ cup chicken broth or water

¼ cup dry white wine

Salt and freshly ground black pepper, to taste

¼ cup Seasoned Bread Crumbs (page 49)

Preheat the broiler.

Heat ¼ cup of olive oil in a large, ovenproof skillet over medium flame. Add the garlic and sauté for I minute, or until lightly golden. Add the sliced peppers and sauté for 2 minutes. Add the anchovies, capers, olives, basil, oregano, broth, and wine to the skillet and cook, stirring occasionally, until all ingredients are blended, about 3 to 4 minutes. Add salt and pepper to taste.

Sprinkle the bread crumbs on top of the pepper mixture and drizzle with about 2 tablespoons olive oil. Broil for 2 to 3 minutes, or until lightly browned.

PALLE DI RISO
(RICE BALLS)

HERE'S A DISH THAT'S MORE POPULAR IN VENICE THAN IN THE SOUTH OF Italy, but we've come to love it. In Venice it's served as part of an antipasto selection.

MAKES 15 TO 18

1 cup converted rice

¾ cup (about ⅓ pound) diced mozzarella

¾ cup grated Parmigiano-Reggiano

4 large fresh basil leaves, chopped

4 eggs, lightly beaten

1 teaspoon salt

¼ teaspoon freshly ground black pepper

1½ cups plain bread crumbs

Olive oil, for frying (about 2 cups)

Rinse the rice and drain it well. Bring 4 cups of water to a boil in a large saucepan. Add the rice and cook for 17 minutes or until done. Drain immediately.

In a large bowl, combine the hot cooked rice, mozzarella, Parmigiano-Reggiano, and basil. Stir gently to combine. Allow to cool for 15 minutes. Add half the beaten eggs and stir rapidly to prevent the eggs from scrambling. Add the salt and pepper.

Spread the rice mixture on a cookie sheet. Cool in the refrigerator for at least 2 hours, or until thoroughly chilled.

When rice has cooled, dampen your hands and roll the rice mixture into 2-inch balls. Wet your hands after forming each ball, to prevent the rice from sticking. Roll the rice balls in the remaining beaten eggs and coat with the bread crumbs.

Heat 2 inches of oil in a deep skillet to a frying temperature of 375°F. (or until a bread crumb sizzles and browns immediately when dropped in). Keeping the oil hot at all times over medium-high heat, fry the rice balls in small batches, turning to brown on all sides, about 3 to 4 minutes. Remove with a slotted spoon or tongs and drain on paper towels. Serve warm.

"*I*'ve been going to Patsy's since I was a kid. Where can you find better Italian food in the Neapolitan tradition? I plan to buy copies of *Patsy's Cookbook* for each of my ten grandchildren to make sure the tradition stays alive in my family."

—JOHN J. PROFACI, HONORARY TRUSTEE, CULINARY
INSTITUTE OF AMERICA, PRESIDENT, COLAVITA USA

Stanley Kay

"I've been going to Patsy's for years, starting when I was a drummer in Buddy Rich's band, and later a drummer for Josephine Baker," recounts Stanley Kay, personal manager and entertainment director for the New York Yankees. "I moved on to become a personal manager for Buddy Rich, Michelle Lee, Gregory Hines, and Maurice Hines. No matter where my career takes me, whether it's show business or sports, Patsy's is still my place, the restaurant I go to with friends and clients. I knew Patsy—father of Joe, grandfather of Sal. And I want to say that his food was as wonderful as his heart—and that was pretty wonderful. And I'm happy to say that nothing has changed."

Jerry Castle AND Cary Grant

"I met Patsy when I was eight years old," Jerry Castle remembers. "My father and uncle took me to the Villanova Restaurant, where Patsy was a waiter and then a manager. Through the years, we followed him to his restaurant Sorrento on West Forty-ninth Street, and then the restaurant on West Fifty-sixth Street down the block from where Patsy's is now. I loved the place then and I love it now. I brought in a lot of people: George Barry, head of the Fabergé Company; Elliott Hyman from Warner Bros.; Jerry and Eileen Ford from the Ford Modeling Agency; Angel Cordero, the jockey; and Johnny Meyers, who brought in Ari Onassis. Onassis really loved Patsy's.

"Everyone was friendly, including Frank Sinatra, who called me Mr. Jerry while I called him Mr. Frank. One of my special friends was Cary Grant; our kids were friends. One night when we were there together, Cary could see I was really blue. When he asked me what was wrong, I told him that my wife had said she wanted a divorce. I told Cary that she had called me a social misfit, and had said that I would never have any friends if it weren't for her.

"Cary said, 'Jerry, I'm your friend, and I'll be your friend until the day I die. And I want you to know that my wife divorced me for the same reason—she also said I was a social misfit, and that I'd never have any friends if it weren't for her.' Cary Grant! Can you believe that? And then he took a pair of cufflinks that he was wearing in his shirt and gave them to me, to commemorate our friendship, he said.

"That kind of thing could happen only at Patsy's—everyone was there, Carmine de Sapio and a whole bunch of politicos. And then there was the time I brought in Teddy Forstmann, you know, from Wall Street. And he told me that he only liked Chinese food. 'Give me a break,' I said, 'try some great Italian food.'

"Anyway, I told one of the Scognamillos about that when I made the reservation. When we came in and sat down to dinner, the waiters came out of the kitchen with a whole bunch of covered dishes and put them in front of Teddy. What was in them? Chinese food that Patsy or Joe had ordered from Shun Lee. Talk about doing anything to make your customers happy. Me, I was more than happy with one of Patsy's great shrimp dishes. And you know, Teddy tried what I was eating, and that was the night he learned to like Italian food."

SHRIMP WITH SAUTÉED FENNEL OVER MESCLUN SALAD

FENNEL IS A POPULAR VEGETABLE IN ITALY, WHERE IT IS EATEN BOTH RAW and cooked. Cooking fennel softens its licorice-like flavor. Try to find small, young fennel, usually available in the spring. This is the best fennel for salads, with a more delicate texture. But I use whatever fennel is available, toning down the stronger flavors of large fennel by cooking it.

SERVES 4

¼ cup olive oil

16 jumbo shrimp, peeled and deveined

1 small fennel bulb

⅓ cup fish broth or chicken broth

1 teaspoon anise liquor (such as pastis or
 Pernod)

Salt and freshly ground black pepper,
 to taste

Mesclun Salad with Vinaigrette
 (page 71)

Heat the olive oil in a large nonstick skillet over medium-high flame. Add the shrimp and sauté until lightly browned on all sides, about 3 minutes. Remove from the skillet and reserve.

Cut off and discard the top of the fennel and any wilted outer leaves. Cut the bulb in half and remove and discard the core. Cut into thin, vertical slices. Wash thoroughly, drain, and set aside.

Add the sliced fennel to the skillet and sauté for 4 to 5 minutes, stirring occasionally. Return the cooked shrimp to the skillet, add the broth, and bring to a simmer. Cover and cook for 3 to 4 minutes, or until most of the broth has evaporated. Add the liquor, stir, and season to taste with salt and pepper. Remove from heat after 1 minute.

Toss the mesclun salad with the vinaigrette and arrange on a serving platter or on 4 individual plates. Spoon shrimp, fennel, and sauce over the salad.

TOMATO BRUSCHETTA

TOMATO BRUSCHETTA WAS ORIGINALLY A POOR MAN'S DISH—A WAY TO stretch stale bread and cheap, bountiful tomatoes into a snack or even a light meal. Today, it has become a prelude to many an elegant dinner. I use plum tomatoes when preparing this dish. The tomatoes are available year-round and contain just enough liquid. Serve with bread or Friselle (page 45).

MAKES 2 TO 3 CUPS

2 pounds ripe plum tomatoes, coarsely chopped

6 scallions (white and green parts), thinly sliced

4 garlic cloves, crushed through a press

¼ cup chopped fresh basil

6 tablespoons olive oil

2 tablespoons balsamic vinegar

Salt and freshly ground black pepper, to taste

1 Italian baguette (about 1 pound), cut into 1-inch slices and lightly toasted

In a large bowl, toss the tomatoes, scallions, garlic, and basil.

Place the oil and vinegar in a screw-top jar. Close tightly and shake until thoroughly combined. Spoon the dressing gradually over the tomato mixture, tossing gently so that vegetables are coated. Season to taste with salt and pepper. Cover and allow to rest for 1 hour.

Uova
DI PURGATORIO

What a name for a dish: Eggs in Purgatory! I was talking about it with Nancy Sinatra Sr., and she likes it as much as I do. It's a simple dish, a real Neapolitan specialty, created by people who learned to make something delicious with a small amount of food, which a lot of people had to do in southern Italy. The dish consists of eggs, either poached or scrambled, in a small amount of spicy sauce. It's a great first course, and I've discovered another use for it: When I'm on the road, doing food demonstrations with Patsy's sauces, I frequently have to make early-morning appearances. And I've learned that not too many people are in the mood for a plate of pasta at 9:00 A.M. So I scramble eggs and cook them in Fra Diavolo sauce. It's a great and delicious surprise. Try it some morning in place of toast or cereal—it spices up the whole day!

Neil Sedaka

"I've enjoyed so many family dinners at Patsy's. I'm always made to feel so comfortable—it's as though I was visiting a friend's home for dinner. And I appreciate the way the Scognamillos remember my likes and dislikes. They're so gracious, the food is wonderful, and the service is always excellent. If I had to pick a favorite dish, I guess it's Patsy's Veal Parmigiana."

VEGETABLE NAPOLEON

ITALIANS LOVE VEGETABLES, AND THIS DISH COMBINES FOUR FAVORITES: eggplant, zucchini, spinach, and peppers. Served in small slices, it's an excellent first course, and it can also take a place as a side dish with chicken or veal. For a lighter version, you can grill or broil the eggplant and zucchini (brushed with a little oil, but not floured) instead of frying.

SERVES 10

¼ cup all-purpose flour

1 medium eggplant (about 1¼ pounds), ends trimmed, peeled, and cut into ¼-inch-thick slices

2 eggs, lightly beaten

½ cup olive oil

2 medium zucchini (about 1 pound), ends trimmed, sliced into ½-inch rounds

1 pound spinach, washed and trimmed

3 garlic cloves, minced

2 tablespoons butter, for greasing pan

½ cup dry bread crumbs

2 teaspoons salt

1 teaspoon freshly ground black pepper

4 cups Tomato Sauce (page 105)

2 Roasted Red Bell Peppers (page 52), cut into ¼-inch strips

1 pound mozzarella, diced into small cubes

½ cup freshly grated Parmigiano-Reggiano

¼ cup chopped fresh basil

Spread the flour on a large plate. Lightly coat the eggplant slices with flour and then dip in the beaten eggs. Heat ¼ cup of the oil in a large nonstick skillet over medium-high flame. Fry the eggplant slices, turning to cook on both sides, until lightly browned, about 5 minutes. Remove, place on paper towels to drain, and reserve.

Add the remaining ¼ cup of oil and the zucchini to the skillet and sauté until just lightly browned, about 5 minutes. Remove zucchini and place on paper towels to drain.

Meanwhile, bring 2 cups of water to a boil in a pot fitted with a steamer insert. Chop the spinach, add to the steamer, cover tightly, and steam for 3 minutes. Drain and press out as much water as possible. Add more oil to the skillet if necessary. Over medium heat, sauté the steamed spinach with the minced garlic until the spinach is just tender, about 3 minutes. Remove from the skillet and place on paper towels to drain.

Preheat the oven to 400°F.

Butter the bottom and insides of a nonstick loaf pan, about 9 × 13 inches. Lightly coat with the bread crumbs.

While building the Napoleon, season each vegetable layer with salt and pepper. Begin by placing a layer of the cooked eggplant atop the bread crumbs. Spoon ¼ cup (4 tablespoons) of tomato sauce over the eggplant, followed by a layer of the cooked zucchini, the red pepper, spinach, and mozzarella, moistening each layer with some sauce and a sprinkling of Parmigiano-Reggiano, bread crumbs, and basil. The final layer should be eggplant, finished with sauce.

Cover the pan with aluminum foil and bake for 35 to 40 minutes, or until all ingredients are heated through. Allow to cool, then refrigerate for at least 6 hours (preferably overnight) to firmly set before unmolding.

When ready to serve, remove the foil and run a knife along the inside edge of the pan. Place a serving dish on top of the pan and quickly invert. Spoon additional sauce around the Napoleon and sprinkle generously with grated cheese before serving.

Al Pacino
WE'RE THE ONE AND ONLY

"For many years I've had the pleasure of dining at my favorite Italian restaurant, Patsy's. The food is simply the best, and I always recommend it to my friends who might not have heard of Patsy's Restaurant. Patsy's was also mentioned in *The God-father,* the book written by Mario Puzo.

"At home, we use Patsy's delicious sauces in all their varieties without fail. I've never heard of any Patsy's eatery except the one owned and operated by my friends on West Fifty-sixth Street in Manhattan."

2

"ITALIANS ARE KNOWN FOR THEIR WONDERFUL SALADS AND vegetables," says Joe. "Bill Boggs orders a Tricolore Salad whenever he comes in, and the Chopped Salad is also a big favorite. Frank Sinatra loved our Broccoli Rabe Affogato, as did another singer—maybe you've heard of Enrico Caruso? My father took care of him at the Villanova. I think the reason Italian vegetable dishes are so delicious is because they're prepared with a light touch—they're not smothered in sauces, no cups of cream, the way they are in some other cuisines.

"At Patsy's, we go along with the Italian idea of letting the vegetables speak for themselves; they're visible, recognizable, and delicious. I must tell you that when we prepared the Broccoli Rabe for Frank, we sautéed the garlic and then removed the cloves before continuing with the dish. Frank liked a mild garlic flavor, but he didn't want to be faced with whole garlic cloves. This is a good idea for anyone who's cooking for people who want only a little garlic in their food. I find it's easy to please guests when you know what they like."

SALADS AND VEGETABLES

BASIC
VINAIGRETTE

INGREDIENTS FOR SALAD DRESSINGS CAN BE WHISKED TOGETHER IN A bowl or shaken up in a cruet. But I suggest using a screw-top jar because it makes blending easier.

MAKES 1 CUP

¾ cup extra-virgin olive oil

¼ cup balsamic vinegar

1 garlic clove, minced

1 tablespoon finely chopped fresh basil
    (about 4 leaves)

Salt and freshly ground black pepper,
    to taste

Place all ingredients in a screw-top jar. Close tightly and shake until thoroughly blended.

"*My Mother,* THE BARTENDER"

"My mother," says Joe, "a soft-spoken, elegant lady, was also a great bartender. When my father opened his first restaurant, they couldn't afford a big staff. So my mother learned how to mix drinks—and she was good at it. Good enough to teach Frank Sinatra when he would come in and help out at the bar—that was in the early days. He would answer the phone, take reservations, and make drinks if my mother was busy showing someone to a table.

"She also taught my nephew, Frank, how to make drinks. Now, if the bartender has to step away or is busy, Frank will pitch in. Not too long ago, I heard someone ask him how he could make such perfect Cosmopolitans—not only were they delicious, he had measured so perfectly there wasn't a drop left in the cocktail shaker. 'My grandmother Concetta taught me,' Frank said, 'and she hated waste.'"

WHITE BEAN AND
SCALLION SALAD

TRADITIONALLY, THIS SALAD IS PREPARED WITH WHITE BEANS. BUT IF you're planning to serve eight or more people, you can make a more colorful presentation by combining the white beans with other varieties: black and pinto beans, for example. In the restaurant, we cook the beans from scratch, but for the home cook I recommend using cooked canned beans.

SERVES 4

1 16-ounce can cannellini or small white beans, rinsed and drained

4 scallions (green and white parts), thinly sliced

1 garlic clove, minced

2 tablespoons chopped fresh flat-leaf parsley

4 tablespoons olive oil

1 tablespoon balsamic vinegar

Salt and freshly ground black pepper, to taste

In a medium serving bowl, combine the drained beans with the scallions, garlic, and parsley.

Combine the oil and vinegar in a screw-top jar. Close the jar tightly and shake until thoroughly combined. Pour the dressing over the bean mixture gradually, stirring, until ingredients are evenly coated. Season to taste with salt and pepper.

GREEN BEAN, POTATO, AND TOMATO SALAD

THIS SALAD MAY BE PREPARED WITH ANY FRESH GREEN BEANS AVAILABLE in your market, but the thin French green beans, also called haricots verts, have the most delicate taste and texture.

SERVES 4

1 pound green beans (preferably haricots verts), ends trimmed

2 medium russet potatoes, peeled and cubed

2 medium ripe, firm tomatoes, each cut into 8 wedges

1 small red onion, thinly sliced

¼ cup chopped fresh basil

Salt and freshly ground black pepper, to taste

¾ cup extra-virgin olive oil

½ cup red wine vinegar

1 garlic clove, minced

Bring a large pot of water to a rolling boil. Add the green beans and cook until just tender, about 5 minutes. Drain in a colander and place under cold running water until beans are cool. Reserve.

Meanwhile, place the potatoes in a medium saucepan, add cold water to cover, and bring to a boil. Cook for 15 to 20 minutes, or until tender when pierced with a fork. Drain in a colander and place under cold running water until potatoes are cool.

Place the green beans, potatoes, tomatoes, onion, and basil in a salad bowl. Season to taste with salt and pepper.

Combine the oil, vinegar, and garlic in a screw-top jar or cruet. Close the jar tightly or place a stopper in the cruet, and shake until thoroughly mixed. Spoon the dressing gradually over the salad, tossing to combine. Refrigerate the salad for 1 to 2 hours before serving.

CHOPPED SALAD

WHY CHOPPED SALAD AT PATSY'S? BECAUSE SO MANY OF OUR CUSTOMERS requested this dish that we decided to add it to our menu. Why did this dish suddenly become so popular? I can only think that it represents comfort food to many. It certainly goes back to a time when the only lettuce that most people knew about was iceberg—still, by the way, the most popular lettuce in the United States.

SERVES 4

1 small head iceberg lettuce, rinsed and coarsely chopped

2 medium ripe, firm tomatoes, chopped

4 anchovy fillets, drained from oil and chopped

½ cup pimiento peppers, chopped

Salt and freshly ground black pepper, to taste

½ cup extra-virgin olive oil

¼ cup red wine vinegar

1 garlic clove, minced

1 tablespoon chopped fresh flat-leaf parsley

Pinch of dried oregano

Place the lettuce, tomatoes, anchovies, and pimientos in a salad bowl. Sprinkle with salt and pepper.

Combine the oil, vinegar, garlic, parsley, oregano, salt, and pepper in a screw-top jar or cruet. Cover tightly and shake until thoroughly blended. Spoon the dressing gradually over salad, mixing to combine.

FENNEL AND ENDIVE
WITH BLOOD ORANGE SEGMENTS

BLOOD ORANGES, THE FRUIT WITH SCARLET FLESH AND A TANGY FLAVOR, have always been popular in Italy. At one time, most blood oranges were grown in Sicily and were an imported and expensive delicacy in the United States. But then came that great garden known as California, and now blood oranges grown there are available at a more reasonable price. This salad may also be prepared with Valencia or navel oranges, but blood oranges provide a livelier flavor and a wonderful contrast of color.

SERVES 4

2 heads endive

2 small bulbs fennel

2 blood oranges

⅓ cup Basic Vinaigrette (page 66)

Salt and freshly ground pepper, to taste

Trim and discard the ends of the endive. Rinse, drain, and cut crosswise into 2-inch pieces.

Cut off and discard the tops of the fennel; remove and discard the wilted outer leaves. Cut the bulbs into thin vertical strips. Rinse and drain.

Peel and separate the oranges into segments.

Combine the endive, fennel, and orange segments in a salad bowl. Spoon dressing over the ingredients and toss to combine. Season to taste with salt and pepper.

MESCLUN SALAD

WITH VINAIGRETTE

I LIKE THE ASSORTMENT OF DELICATE GREENS PROVIDED BY MESCLUN.
This light salad makes an excellent introduction to a main course of fish.

SERVES 4

½ pound mesclun greens (about 3 cups),
    rinsed and dried

1 tablespoon finely chopped fresh basil
    (about 4 leaves)

2 ripe tomatoes, quartered

4 tablespoons olive oil

1 tablespoon balsamic vinegar

2 garlic cloves, crushed through a press

Salt and freshly ground black pepper,
    to taste

Place the mesclun in a salad bowl and add the basil and tomatoes.

Combine the oil, vinegar, and garlic in a screw-top jar. Close the jar tightly and shake until thoroughly blended. Spoon the dressing gradually over the salad, tossing gently to coat all ingredients. Season with salt and pepper.

David Brown

Movie producer David Brown discloses, "I've been going to Patsy's Restaurant since 1964. Why am I such a fan of the place? Because Patsy's is predictable. By that I mean predictably good. I know that I can rely on a consistently delicious meal. If you ask me what's my favorite dish, I have to say it's whatever I ate the last time I was there. Everything is so right at Patsy's, including the melon served with prosciutto—Patsy's melons are ripe even in January. I go there as often as I can, and I enjoy sitting upstairs where Frank Sinatra sat. Patsy's gives great parties, too. The last one Helen [Gurley Brown] and I went to was for Rosemary Clooney—we had a great time. We always do at Patsy's."

RICOTTA SALATA SALAD

RICOTTA SALATA IS THE DRY VERSION OF THE USUALLY SOFT AND CREAMY ricotta cheese. It has a slight tang and a crumbly texture. It adds interest to a salad, or it can be enjoyed as an appetizer served with tomatoes and a crusty slice of pane di casa or ciabatta.

SERVES 4

½ pound mesclun greens (about 3 cups), rinsed and dried

4 ripe plum tomatoes, chopped

16 gaeta olives, pitted and chopped

½ pound ricotta salata, crumbled

½ cup Basic Vinaigrette (page 66)

Place the mesclun, tomatoes, olives, and ricotta salata in a large salad bowl. Spoon vinaigrette over salad and toss to combine.

Lionel

"Joe Scognamillo is not just a successful restaurateur, he's my brother," claims nationally syndicated talk-show host Lionel. "His family embraced me upon my arrival in New York, and I will never forget him and them for that. The food is beyond delicious. His toothsome viands and victuals are nonpareil in New York. The care and attention Joe and his family pay to the quality of their food are so easily seen in the very dishes themselves. Sal gives birth to foods, he doesn't just cook. Rosie makes you feel that you're in her house—as you are. Anna is most precious. Frank is the brother you never had. I love Patsy's as they have loved me."

ASPARAGUS WITH PANCETTA

PANCETTA IS ITALY'S VERSION OF BACON. IT'S THE SAME CUT OF PORK, BUT it's cured with salt and spices rather than smoked. This recipe is my one and only foray into fusion cooking—it calls for Chinese oyster sauce. What would Grandfather Patsy have said? "As long as it makes your customers happy." I can hear him now.

SERVES 4

6 slices pancetta (about ⅛ pound), finely chopped

2 tablespoons olive oil

4 garlic cloves, minced

1½ pounds asparagus, cooked (see headnote on page 38)

Freshly ground black pepper, to taste

¼ cup chopped fresh flat-leaf parsley

2 tablespoons oyster sauce

Sauté the pancetta in a large skillet over medium heat until brown and slightly crisp, about 5 minutes. Remove from the skillet and reserve.

Discard the rendered pancetta fat from skillet, add the olive oil, and heat over medium flame until shimmering. Add the garlic and sauté, stirring constantly, until just golden, about 30 seconds. Return the reserved pancetta to the skillet and add the cooked asparagus, pepper, parsley, and ¼ cup water. Bring to a boil, reduce the heat to low, cover, and simmer for 1 to 3 minutes, until all ingredients are heated through. Stir in the oyster sauce, increase the flame to high, bring the sauce to a boil, and cook for 1 minute. Serve hot.

ASPARAGUS
PARMIGIANO
WITH BASIL

A SIMPLE AND SATISFYING DISH. ADD A BIT OF CHOPPED BASIL TO MAKE IT more interesting. I find that it contrasts perfectly with the asparagus and cheese.

SERVES 4

1½ pounds asparagus, washed and trimmed

2 tablespoons butter

½ teaspoon salt

¼ teaspoon freshly ground black pepper

¼ cup minced fresh basil

¾ cup freshly grated Parmigiano-Reggiano

Preheat the broiler.

Place the asparagus in a large skillet in one layer. Add water almost to cover and bring to a boil. Lower the heat to a simmer, cover, and cook asparagus until crisp-tender, approximately 5 to 10 minutes (time will depend on freshness and thickness of asparagus). Remove from the skillet and place in a baking pan with ¼ cup of the cooking water.

In a small saucepan, melt the butter over low heat. Drizzle the asparagus with the melted butter, season with salt and pepper, and top with the basil and Parmigiano-Reggiano. Broil for 3 to 5 minutes, or until all ingredients are hot and the cheese is lightly browned.

BROCCOLI RABE AFFOGATO

I'M THE FIRST ONE TO ADMIT THAT BROCCOLI RABE CAN BE WONDERFUL OR terrible, and there's no way to tell when purchasing this vegetable. It can have just enough bitterness to make life interesting, but some broccoli rabe is too strong. I have found that quick cooking for this temperamental green is best. Cooked for longer than 15 minutes, the bitterness is intensified. If all this sounds like too much trouble, substitute regular broccoli.

SERVES 4

2 bunches of broccoli rabe
   (about 2 pounds)
⅓ cup olive oil

6 garlic cloves, halved
½ teaspoon crushed red pepper flakes
Salt, to taste

Trim the broccoli rabe, removing the tough stems and discarding wilted leaves or any leaves with yellow buds. Rinse the remaining leaves and drain.

Heat the oil in a large nonstick skillet over medium flame. Add the garlic and sauté until lightly browned, about 2 minutes. Add the broccoli rabe, red pepper flakes, and 2½ cups of water. Bring to a boil, cover, reduce the heat to low, and simmer for 10 to 15 minutes, or until the broccoli rabe is tender. Season to taste with salt, and serve with the cooking liquid.

EGGPLANT PARMIGIANA

HERE'S EVERYONE'S FAVORITE. I HAD TO INCLUDE THIS RECIPE BECAUSE so many of Patsy's customers have told me that this is the first dish they ate when introduced to Italian cooking, and it's still the dish they like best.

SERVES 4 TO 6

1 large eggplant (about 1¼ pounds)

½ cup all-purpose flour

3 large eggs, lightly beaten

1½ cups dry bread crumbs

¾ cup olive oil

3 cups Tomato Sauce (page 105)

½ pound mozzarella, diced into small pieces

¼ cup freshly grated Parmigiano-Reggiano

Preheat the oven to 400°F.

Peel the eggplants, remove the ends, and slice into ¼-inch rounds. Put the flour on a large plate, the eggs in a shallow bowl, and the bread crumbs on a second large plate. Coat each eggplant slice in the flour, then the beaten eggs, and then the bread crumbs. Shake to remove excess coating.

Heat the oil in a large nonstick skillet over medium flame. Sauté the eggplant, a few slices at a time without crowding the pan, turning to brown on both sides, about 3 to 4 minutes. (When cooking in batches, be sure to keep the oil hot, and add more if necessary.) Place fried eggplant slices on paper towels to absorb excess oil.

Spoon ½ cup of the tomato sauce on the bottom of a 10 × 8 × 2-inch baking pan. Place half the eggplant slices in the pan, and top with half the remaining sauce, half the mozzarella, and half the grated Parmigiano. Cover with remaining eggplant and layer on the remaining sauce, mozzarella, and Parmigiano. Spoon ¼ cup water around the inside edges of the baking pan. Bake uncovered in the preheated oven for 20 minutes, or until all the ingredients are heated through and the cheese has melted.

Alec Baldwin

"I come to Patsy's whenever I'm in New York. At Patsy's you feel as though you're eating in someone's home. All the staff is friendly, and I like to go there with my friends and family for a great, home-cooked meal—that's what it's like. My favorite dish is the Eggplant Parmigiana. And the desserts are not just good—they're *too* good."

"*M*usic gypsies such as myself wander around the world always looking, but seldom finding a place of comfort, especially in the gastronomic world. I've slaved here at Carnegie Hall for the last twenty years and enjoyed the cuisine of, as we say 'the one, the *only* Patsy's.' Long may it live!"

—SKITCH HENDERSON

CAVOLFIORE FRITTO

I MAKE THIS DISH ESPECIALLY FOR THOSE PEOPLE WHO SAY THAT THEY hate cauliflower, would never eat cauliflower, and can't stand cauliflower. Prepared this way, I've seen it change many a cauliflower hater into a cauliflower lover. I think the secret is not to overcook this vegetable, which has its own form of delicacy, despite its sturdy appearance.

SERVES 4

1 medium cauliflower (about 2 pounds), separated into florets

2 cups all-purpose flour, sifted

¼ cup milk

1 teaspoon salt

½ teaspoon freshly ground black pepper

Pinch of baking powder

2 eggs, lightly beaten

Olive oil, for frying (about 2 cups)

Bring a large pot of water to a boil. Add the cauliflower and cook for 4 minutes; it should remain firm. Drain in a colander, then return to the pot and fill with cold water. Allow the cauliflower to remain in water until cool enough to handle. Drain and place florets on paper towels to absorb excess water.

In a large bowl, combine 2 cups flour with 1¼ cups water and the milk, salt, pepper, and baking powder. Mix well. Add the eggs and stir to combine. The mixture should have the consistency of pancake batter. If the mixture is too thick, thin with a small amount of water; if too thin, add more flour. Add the drained cauliflower and toss until each floret is coated with batter. Shake off excess.

Heat 3 inches of oil in a deep skillet to a frying temperature of 375°F. Add 1 or 2 drops of batter to the oil; when it sizzles and rises to the top the oil is ready. Keeping the oil hot at all times, cook the cauliflower quickly in small batches for 2 to 3 minutes, turning to brown on all sides. Remove from the oil and drain on paper towels. Serve warm.

SAUTÉED MUSHROOMS WITH COGNAC AND CABERNET SAUVIGNON

I ORIGINALLY PREPARED THIS DISH FOR A CUSTOMER WHO ASKED FOR mushrooms. "Not plain mushrooms," he said, "mushrooms gussied up." So I gussied, and this is the result. They go especially well with a small steak or over pasta.

SERVES 4

1 pound fresh white mushrooms, cleaned
  and thinly sliced

¼ cup olive oil

10 garlic cloves, thinly sliced

1 tablespoon chopped fresh basil

¼ cup Cognac

¼ cup Cabernet Sauvignon

¼ cup light cream

1 tablespoon butter

Salt and freshly ground black pepper,
  to taste

Bring 1 quart of water to a boil in a large saucepan. Add the sliced mushrooms, blanch for 2 minutes, then drain and run under cold water to stop cooking. Reserve.

Heat the oil in a large skillet over medium flame and sauté the garlic until lightly browned, about 2 minutes. Remove with a slotted spoon and reserve. Add the blanched mushrooms to the skillet and sauté over high heat for 3 to 4 minutes, or until mushrooms begin to brown. Remove from the heat. Add the cooked garlic, basil, Cognac, Cabernet Sauvignon, cream, butter, and ¼ cup of water. Stir to combine, return to the heat, and bring to a boil over high flame. Reduce the heat to low and simmer for 3 minutes, or until sauce thickens slightly. Season to taste with salt and pepper.

BAKED MUSHROOMS WITH ZUCCHINI STUFFING

IF YOU'VE SPENT ANY TIME IN ITALY, YOU KNOW ITALIANS HAVE A PENCHANT for stuffed vegetables. Here's a great example.

MAKES 24, SERVES 6

½ cup canned chopped tomatoes with juice

¼ cup olive oil, plus more for coating baking dish

1 medium yellow onion, finely chopped (about ½ cup)

2 garlic cloves, finely chopped

3 medium zucchini (about 1¼ pounds), rinsed and finely diced

1 tablespoon chopped fresh basil

1 tablespoon chopped fresh flat-leaf parsley

1½ teaspoons salt

¾ teaspoon freshly ground black pepper

½ cup dry bread crumbs

½ cup freshly grated Parmigiano-Reggiano

1 egg, lightly beaten

24 jumbo white mushrooms (about 1 pound), rinsed and patted dry

Preheat the oven to 450°F.

Place the tomatoes in a small saucepan and bring to a simmer over medium heat. Cook for 10 minutes, remove from the heat, and reserve.

Heat ¼ cup of the olive oil in a large saucepan over medium flame. Add the onion and garlic and sauté, stirring, for 3 minutes, or until lightly browned. Add the diced zucchini and continue cooking until lightly browned. Stir in the reserved tomatoes, the basil, parsley, 1 teaspoon salt, and ½ teaspoon pepper. Remove from the heat and cool.

In a large mixing bowl, combine the bread crumbs and cheese. Add the cooled zucchini mixture and the beaten egg, stirring until all ingredients are thoroughly combined.

Lightly coat a baking dish with oil. Place the mushrooms cap side down in one layer in the dish. Season with the remaining salt and pepper, and fill with the zucchini mixture. Bake in the oven for 20 to 25 minutes, or until a light crust forms. Serve hot.

"GENTLEMEN I HAVE KNOWN"

"Most people didn't know that Carroll O'Connor spoke fluent Italian," says Rose. "He lived in Italy when he wasn't making movies, and he spoke such perfect Italian it was hard to believe he wasn't Italian. He carried around a tape recorder into which he would ask you to say your name, so that he could get the pronunciation absolutely right.

"Tony Bennett did a wonderful sketch of Joe (below), which I have framed. He's so appreciative of everything at Patsy's, and he talks about his mother, who first brought him to Patsy's when he was a kid. My family is Italian, so it's part of my heritage to like people who care about their mothers. Joe and I appeared with Tony on Robin Leach's television show, *Lifestyles of the Rich and the Famous*—that was fun. Frank Sinatra and Tony had a lot of respect for each other; it was touching that day at Patsy's when Nancy Sinatra gave Tony her father's briefcase, after they announced that they were planning to create the Frank Sinatra School of the Arts. Tony spearheaded the movement to get a school named after his dear friend Frank Sinatra. Nancy Sinatra wanted to thank him, and looking around she said she saw her father's personal attaché case and she gave it to Tony, who wouldn't let anyone else carry it during the remainder of the party.

"Alec Baldwin came in one night with his father, sister, and Kim Basinger, and he told me that he was trying hard to quit smoking. His father had brought him honey-roasted nuts, which he had prepared, hoping Alec would munch on the nuts instead of lighting up. Alec insisted on sharing those with me. 'I know you don't smoke, Rose,' he said, 'but they're so delicious I want you to have some.'"

THANKS FOR ALL THE GREAT FOOD—

Lucille Ball AND THE OTHER KIDS

"My mother was crazy about Lucille Ball," says Anna. "She just loved that Lucy show. So one day when Lucy's husband, Gary, was at the restaurant having lunch, I told him that he had to do me a favor—he had to bring Lucille Ball to the restaurant.

"So one night, Gary comes in with Lucille, and my mother was hostessing upstairs. I called her and said I was sending two for dinner, but I didn't tell her who it was. There was my mother at the top of the stairs, and when she saw Lucille Ball coming up, she screamed, 'Lucy! Lucy!'—we could hear her all through the restaurant.

"My mother was crazy about Lucille Ball, and Lucille Ball was crazy about my mother. One Saturday Lucille was at our restaurant, and it was the day before Mother's Day. 'I won't see you tomorrow,' she said, 'because my daughter wants to take me to Tavern on the Green for Mother's Day.'

"So I said, 'Okay, have a nice Mother's Day.'

"Well, the next day, who walks into Patsy's but Lucille Ball. I asked her how come—she was supposed to be at another restaurant. She said, 'I'd rather come here and see your mother.'

"Her daughter Lucie Arnaz came to Patsy's when she was in a Neil Simon play on Broadway. A lot of young actors came in when they were starting out in New York. Matthew Broderick was here, as was Tom Hanks, who got engaged at Patsy's.

"A lot of show people would bring their kids here: Frank Sinatra, of course, Jerry Stiller and Anne Meara come regularly with Ben Stiller and Amy, Nick Clooney—that's Rosemary's brother—comes in with George Clooney, and Dean Martin and Lou Costello used to bring their daughters, Deana and Chris. Gregory Peck came with his kids when they were in town. The last time Gregory Peck was in, I asked how come I never saw his kids anymore. 'Anna,' Gregory said, 'when Poppa pays, the kids come. When Poppa doesn't pay, the kids don't come. It's as simple as that.'

"My mother loved all kids—it didn't matter to her if their parents weren't famous. When she'd see a family come in with kids, she'd sit down next to them and play with the kids so that the parents could eat in peace—especially the mothers. And those kids really loved my mother, too.

"I remember one time this family came in, and they had two boys, maybe eight and nine, and they asked for my mother. 'Where's the little lady who's always here?' they asked. The waiter tried to tell them as gently as he could that my mother had passed away, but the boys wouldn't believe him. 'You're fooling us,' they said, and they ran upstairs looking for my mother, and then they ran downstairs. Finally, they came back to the table. 'She's really not here.' And they were sad. The waiter was just as sad. 'I tried to tell you,' he said. Everyone loved my mother."

SAUTÉED
SPINACH

THIS IS AN EASY DISH TO PREPARE AND IS LIKED BY BOTH SPINACH LOVERS and people who thought they hated spinach. The important thing is to make sure that the spinach is completely free of sand. Rinse and drain a few times until there is absolutely no sand left in the bowl.

SERVES 4

2 pounds fresh spinach, stemmed and
  washed thoroughly (see above)
¼ cup olive oil

8 garlic cloves, thinly sliced
Salt and freshly ground black pepper,
  to taste

Bring a large pot of water to a boil and blanch the spinach for 2 minutes. Drain, press out as much water as possible, and reserve.

Heat the olive oil in a large skillet over a low flame and sauté the garlic until golden brown, about 3 minutes. Remove from the heat and add the drained spinach. Toss until evenly coated with the oil, add ½ cup water, and season with salt and pepper. Cover and return to high heat for 2 minutes. Reduce heat to low and simmer for an additional 3 minutes, being careful not to cook off all of the liquid (or the spinach will burn). Serve hot.

FRIED
ZUCCHINI BLOSSOMS

ZUCCHINI BLOSSOMS—THE ORANGE FLOWER FROM THIS MULTIFUNCTIONAL vegetable—are not always available, but when our supplier has them we add them to our menu. They come out crisp and delicious when dipped in this simple batter and fried in hot oil.

SERVES 4

14 to 16 zucchini blossoms
   (about 1 pound)

1 cup warm water (105° to 115°F.)

1 package (2¼ teaspoons) active dried
   yeast

1¼ cups all-purpose flour

½ teaspoon salt, plus more to taste

¼ teaspoon freshly ground black pepper,
   plus more to taste

1 teaspoon chopped fresh flat-leaf
   parsley

Olive oil, for frying (about 2 cups)

Rinse the zucchini blossoms in cold water and drain.

Prepare the batter by placing the warm water in a large mixing bowl and stirring in yeast until dissolved. Set aside in a warm place for 10 minutes. Add the flour and whisk vigorously until smooth. Allow to rest for at least 20 minutes to fully activate the yeast. Stir in the ½ teaspoon salt, ¼ teaspoon pepper, and the parsley, blending to a thick pancake-batter consistency.

Add 2 to 3 inches of oil to a deep fryer or a Dutch oven, and slowly heat to a frying temperature of 375°F. If you don't have a thermometer, spoon one or two drops of batter into the fryer; when it rises to the top add zucchini blossoms. Dip the blossoms in the batter, making sure to coat each flower completely. Keeping the oil hot at all times and working in small batches, place the blossoms in the deep fryer or Dutch oven, turning until golden brown on all sides, about 3 minutes. Drain on paper towels. Season to taste with additional salt and pepper, and serve immediately.

Danny Thomas

"'Joey,' Danny Thomas asked me when he came to Patsy's just after he had appeared on the Donahue show, 'where is my picture? How come it's not up on your Wall of Fame?'

"'Danny,' I answered, 'you ask me that every time you come in here. And every time I tell you that we'd love to put your picture up, if you'd only send us one.'

"Danny laughed, 'You're right. I keep forgetting. But this time I won't forget—I promise I'll get you a picture.'

"We talked a little more, reminisced about mutual friends, and Danny said, 'Isn't it something the way everyone is traveling around? The guys from the Rat Pack are all on the road, Sinatra is doing a world tour. You know why, Joey? Because we're all running away from death, that's why.'

"After lunch we said goodbye, with Danny Thomas promising yet again to send me his picture.

"A week later he passed away, and Liz Smith wrote a column about him, mentioning the picture he had promised to send us. One month later Marlo Thomas, Danny's daughter, came to Patsy's and handed me a large white envelope.

"'It's my father's picture,' she said, 'the one he wanted to give you. I'm keeping my father's promise.'"

ZUCCHINI A SCAPECE

"HOW CAN I TRANSLATE OR EXPLAIN THE WORD *SCAPECE*?" SAYS JOE. "IT'S dialect, and means something like 'however it goes.' It's a dish best epitomized by a shrug, and expresses a casual attitude. Maybe the best translation of *scapece* is the current slang expression, 'Whatever.' Don't like mint or can't find it, use basil—*whatever*."

SERVES 4

2 medium zucchini, rinsed and dried

½ cup olive oil

Salt and freshly ground black pepper,
    to taste

5 garlic cloves, thinly sliced

¼ cup Basic Vinaigrette (page 66)

10 fresh mint leaves, chopped (fresh basil
    may be substituted)

1 tablespoon chopped fresh flat-leaf
    parsley

Pinch of oregano

Trim and discard the ends of each zucchini, and cut into ¼-inch-thick rounds.

Heat the oil in a large skillet over a medium flame, and sauté the zucchini rounds in batches on both sides until browned, about 7 to 8 minutes. Remove with a slotted spoon and set on paper towels to drain.

Decoratively arrange the warm zucchini rounds in one layer on a large platter. Season with salt and pepper. Alternate raw garlic slices and zucchini, drizzling each time with the vinaigrette. Sprinkle with the mint, parsley, and oregano. Marinate at room temperature for 2 hours, occasionally spooning marinade over the zucchini. Serve at room temperature.

GRANDMA JOSIE'S
ZUCCHINI PIE

MY WIFE'S FAMILY IS AS ITALIAN AS MINE, AND JUST FOR THE FUN OF IT
I'm including her mother's recipe for Zucchini Pie. Josie is Grandma to my kids, and that's
how this recipe got its name. Even though her parents came from Italy, my mother-in-
law loves American food, and she took an Italian favorite vegetable, zucchini, and
topped it with an American standby, a prepared biscuit mix.

SERVES 6 TO 8

2 tablespoons unsalted butter

3 medium zucchini (about 1 pound total),
    sliced ⅛ inch thick

1 teaspoon salt

½ teaspoon freshly ground black pepper

½ pound mozzarella, cubed

½ cup biscuit mix (such as Bisquick)

1 cup whole milk

¼ cup vegetable oil

1 large egg

1 small yellow onion, finely diced

2 tablespoons chopped fresh basil

3 tablespoons freshly grated Parmigiano-
    Reggiano

Preheat the oven to 375°F.

Grease an 8 × 10 × 2-inch baking dish with the butter. Arrange the zucchini slices in
the dish, season with ½ teaspoon salt and ¼ teaspoon pepper, and top with the
mozzarella.

In a medium bowl, combine the biscuit mix, the remaining ½ teaspoon salt and
¼ teaspoon pepper, milk, oil, egg, onion, basil, and Parmigiano-Reggiano. Mix the batter thoroughly and spread over the zucchini and cheese.

Bake in the oven for 45 to 50 minutes. Remove and allow to set 15 to 20 minutes
before serving.

3

"WE ATE A LOT OF SOUPS WHEN WE WERE GROWING UP," says Joe. "They were meals—*main* meals, not just a soup you'd have before your dinner. My mother's soups were filling and delicious, loaded with vegetables. Let's say she'd buy eggplant—a nice, big eggplant; it was cheap in those days. Part of the eggplant might go for an Eggplant Parmigiana, or an Eggplant Sandwich, and the rest of it would go into the soup."

"Whatever vegetables we had in the house, they would be added to the soup," Anna explains. "And there would always be different kinds of beans—white beans, fava beans, lentils, and kidney beans.

"And with the beans in the soup there was also pasta. Back then, pasta was sold in really long strands out of a big barrel. Women would come in to buy a pound or two at a time, and then there were always broken pieces at the bottom of the barrel. My mother and the other women would come in and buy bags of those broken pasta

SOUPS

PASTA E CECI

ESCAROLE IN BRODO

PASTA CON LENTICCHIE

MINESTRONE

PASTA E PISELLI

STRACCIATELLA

ZUCCHINI AND EGG SOUP

pieces—they were perfect for soup, thickened the liquid, and were a lot cheaper than the long strands.

"Today we buy a ready-made product from Italy and it looks like those broken pieces, all different sizes and shapes. But now, of course, it is especially made to look that way. Any small pasta will do for these soups—a tubettini or orzo would also be good. And if you prefer a lighter soup, more of a first course, try the Stracciatella."

PASTA E CECI

"THIS IS ONE OF THE DISHES WE HAD OFTEN AS KIDS," SAYS JOE. "WE ATE lots of chickpeas and pasta. That went far to feed a big family like ours, and we loved it. Years later, we learned that combining chickpeas and lentils with vegetables and maybe a small amount of meat or chicken gave us protein. Not that my mother said that —she just knew what was good by instinct."

"Now," says Anna, "Pasta e Ceci is considered a treat, even a gourmet dish. It's a favorite at the restaurant. When Rosemary Clooney was in the hospital, she would send her husband to Patsy's for large containers of this soup. And it is more than a soup— served with some crusty bread, it's a meal in itself. It was a meal for us when we were growing up."

Here's an easy way to prepare Pasta e Ceci at home, made with canned cooked chickpeas. You come home from work and need a fast meal, this is it. It's especially good on a cold night.

SERVES 6

⅓ cup olive oil

1 medium yellow onion, diced

2 stalks celery, chopped

1 small carrot, chopped

2 cloves garlic, minced

1 14-ounce can whole plum tomatoes,
 with juice

6 cups vegetable broth or water

1 15-ounce can chickpeas, undrained

½ pound fusilli or ziti pasta, cooked
 al dente

Salt and freshly ground black pepper,
 to taste

¼ cup chopped fresh flat-leaf parsley

Heat the oil in a large saucepan or soup pot over medium-high flame and sauté the onion, celery, and carrot, stirring occasionally, for 3 minutes, or until onions are just translucent. Add the garlic and sauté 1 minute, or until lightly golden.

Coarsely chop the tomatoes and add with their juice to the saucepan. Add the broth or water and bring to a boil. Cover, reduce the heat to low, and simmer for 20 minutes.

Add the chickpeas and the cooked pasta, stir to combine, and simmer for an additional 3 to 5 minutes, or until all ingredients are heated through. Season with salt and pepper. Stir in the parsley and serve hot with thick slices of dense bread.

Rosemary Clooney

"Since 1948, Patsy's is the restaurant I go to the moment I arrive in New York. For the first few years, when times were hard for an aspiring singer, Patsy and Concetta just told me to pay my check when I could, and not to worry if I couldn't. I felt as though I had family in New York. Since then, I've been going to Patsy's with my children and my grandchildren, and they're family to all of us. To me, there is only one Patsy's—it's located on West Fifty-sixth Street and in my heart."

ESCAROLE IN BRODO

IN ITALY, ESCAROLE IS NOT ONLY USED IN SALAD BUT IS ALSO COOKED AS a side dish or in a soup. Depending on the age of the escarole, it can be cooked immediately in the soup or blanched in boiling water for a minute or two to tone down the slightly bitter flavor. How to decide whether to blanch or not to blanch? Pull off a leaf of escarole and taste it. That's always the best test of all.

SERVES 6

1 head escarole (about 1½ pounds)

2 tablespoons olive oil

3 scallions (white and green parts), finely chopped

6 cups chicken broth

Salt and freshly ground black pepper, to taste

¼ cup freshly grated Parmigiano-Reggiano

Trim the base of the escarole and separate into leaves, discarding any wilted or discolored ones. Wash the remaining leaves thoroughly, cut into ribbons, and reserve.

Heat the oil in a soup pot or large saucepan over medium flame, add the scallions, and sauté for 2 minutes, or until lightly browned. Add the reserved escarole and continue to cook and stir for 1 minute.

Add the broth and bring to a boil. Reduce the heat to low, cover, and simmer for 20 to 30 minutes, stirring occasionally, until escarole is tender.

Remove from heat and season with salt and pepper. Stir in the Parmigiano-Reggiano just before serving.

PASTA CON
LENTICCHIE

I'VE COME TO THE CONCLUSION THAT ITALIANS NEVER MET A BEAN THEY didn't like. Fresh, dried, canned, they all have their uses and add depth and heartiness to a dish and a meal. Originally, as my father has said, beans were a large part of the cuisine because combined with pasta they provided a filling and healthful main course. Today, beans are appreciated for flavor, texture, and their ability to round out a dish.

SERVES 10 TO 12

⅓ cup olive oil

3 medium yellow onions, diced

2 cloves garlic, minced

3 cups Tomato Sauce (page 105)

1 pound lentils, picked over and rinsed

½ pound pasta wheels or stars, cooked
   al dente

¼ cup chopped fresh basil

Salt and freshly ground black pepper,
   to taste

Heat the oil in a large saucepan or soup pot over a medium flame and sauté the onions for about 3 minutes, stirring occasionally, or until just browned. Add the garlic and sauté for 1 minute, until lightly golden.

Add the Tomato Sauce to the saucepan. Add the lentils and 12 cups water, and bring to a boil. Cover, reduce the heat to low, and simmer for 40 to 45 minutes, or until the lentils are tender. Add the cooked pasta and simmer for an additional 3 to 5 minutes, or until all ingredients are heated through.

Stir in the basil and season with salt and pepper.

MINESTRONE

THIS IS OUR VERSION OF THE GREAT VEGETABLE SOUP FROM ITALY. MY grandparents came from Naples, and the soup is prepared southern style, with both beans and pasta. In the north of Italy, the starch used is rice. There is an abundance of fresh vegetables in this soup, because as my grandfather said, *"Quello che cimetti, lo ritrovi,"* which means "What you put in, is what you get out." Sometimes literal translations are not too successful, but the general idea is clear: Cook with fine ingredients and you'll have a fine dish. That was my grandfather Patsy's motto more than fifty years ago, and it's our motto today.

SERVES 16 TO 18

½ cup olive oil

2 medium yellow onions, finely chopped

3 celery ribs, finely chopped

4 garlic cloves, minced

1 28-ounce can plum tomatoes, with juice

1 ham bone (optional)

2 medium carrots, diced

2 medium Idaho potatoes, peeled and
    cubed

1 medium cauliflower (about 2 pounds),
    separated into florets

2 medium zucchini, cubed

1 10-ounce package frozen peas, thawed

1 15-ounce can cannellini beans, rinsed
    and drained

¾ pound orzo pasta, cooked al dente

3 tablespoons chopped fresh basil

3 tablespoons chopped fresh flat-leaf
    parsley

Salt and freshly ground black pepper,
    to taste

Heat the oil in a large soup pot over medium-high flame and sauté the onion and celery for 6 to 7 minutes, or until lightly browned. Reduce the heat to low and sauté the garlic until golden, about 1 to 2 minutes. Coarsely chop the tomatoes and add to the pot with their juice. Increase the heat to high and add the ham bone, carrots, potatoes, cauliflower, and 12 cups water. Bring to a boil, reduce the heat to low, cover, and simmer for 15 to 17 minutes.

Add the zucchini, peas, and beans, and bring to a boil again. Reduce the heat to low, cover, and simmer for an additional 15 to 18 minutes. Add the cooked pasta, basil, and parsley, season with salt and pepper to taste, and simmer for an additional 2 minutes, or until the pasta is heated through. Remove the ham bone (if using) and serve.

The Patsy's Tradition

"To my father, his customers came first. That's the way he was," remembers Anna. "John Kluge and I were talking about that. Maybe you know him—he's one of the world's richest men. He also knew my father from the Villanova Restaurant days —my father was a waiter there, and then he became a manager—this was before he opened his first restaurant, the Sorrento. And John Kluge said that my father was always dedicated to the comfort of his customers.

"I remember that better than anyone, because when I got married my father said, 'You better pick a day when the restaurant is closed, or most of the family won't be able to come to your wedding. I'm not going to close the restaurant.'

"'But, Pa,' I said, 'I'm your firstborn daughter—you wouldn't do that to me.'

'I'm telling you,' my father said. I didn't believe him, but the day of my wedding, my brothers couldn't come to the ceremony because they had to be at the restaurant. My parents came—it was at the St. George Hotel in Brooklyn—but my brothers could only come for a late drink after the restaurant was closed. And you know, ever since then, everyone in the family gets married on the Fourth of July, Labor Day, or Thanksgiving, whatever day the restaurant is closed. My father has passed away, but that's still a tradition in the family—well, almost. Sal was married in August because his wife was in the midst of law school and it was the only free time."

PASTA E PISELLI

EXCELLENT FRESH PEAS ARE HARD TO FIND EVEN IN THE MONTH OF JUNE, when peas are supposed to be at their youthful best. That's why this recipe calls for frozen peas, which I've found are usually better than the fresh variety. And much, *much* easier.

SERVES 8

⅓ cup olive oil

1 medium yellow onion, diced

6 scallions (white and green parts), sliced

¼ pound prosciutto, minced

8 cups vegetable broth or water

2 10-ounce packages frozen green peas, thawed

½ pound tubetti or orzo pasta, cooked al dente

2 tablespoons chopped fresh flat-leaf parsley

2 tablespoons chopped fresh basil

Salt and freshly ground black pepper, to taste

Heat the oil in a large saucepan or soup pot over a medium flame and sauté the onion and scallions, stirring occasionally, for about 3 minutes, or until scallions are soft and onions are just translucent. Add the prosciutto and sauté for 2 minutes. Add the broth or water and bring to a boil. Add the thawed peas, reduce the heat to low, cover, and simmer for 30 minutes, or until the peas are tender. Stir in the cooked pasta, parsley, and basil, and season with salt and pepper. Continue simmering for an additional 3 to 5 minutes, or until all ingredients are heated through.

STRACCIATELLA

STRACCIATELLA MEANS "LITTLE RAGS," WHICH DESCRIBES THE APPEARANCE of the eggs cooked in the soup. This is best made with imported angel hair pasta that comes in the form of nests. If you can't find nests, substitute half a pound of angel hair pasta, also called capellini, broken in half.

SERVES 4

- **1 bunch fresh spinach, washed and chopped**
- **6 cups chicken broth**
- **2 angel hair pasta nests (about ½ pound)**
- **2 eggs, lightly beaten**
- **2 tablespoons freshly grated Parmigiano-Reggiano, plus more for garnish**
- **Salt and freshly ground black pepper, to taste**

Bring a large pot of water to a boil, add the spinach, and blanch for 2 minutes. Drain and reserve.

In a large soup pot, bring the broth to a boil, reduce the heat to a simmer, and add the blanched spinach, cooking for 2 to 3 minutes, or until tender. Crush the angel hair pasta nests, add to the boiling broth, and cook for 2 minutes, or until al dente.

While the soup is cooking, combine the eggs and the Parmigiano-Reggiano in a small bowl and mix well. Whisk the egg mixture quickly into the broth and cook for 2 minutes, or until the eggs have formed soft curds. Season to taste with salt and pepper, and serve with additional grated Parmigiano-Reggiano on the side.

Remo Giachino

"I'm a wine importer and distributor, and I've been selling wine to the Scognamillo family ever since Patsy opened his first restaurant," says Remo, a friend of the family for fifty years. "To know the family is to become a friend. Patsy and I, we got to be so close. He was the absolute personification of a gentleman. And in the restaurant, he went around in a gray jacket like a busboy, pitching in, cleaning tables, making sure that everything was okay. He didn't go around in a fancy jacket, like an owner, because he figured the customers wouldn't ask him for a glass of water if he looked like that.

"My company still supplies wine to Patsy's. That's another thing—once the Scognamillos like you and do business with you, they stay with you forever. Let me give you an example: When Frank Sinatra was expected in town, I'd get a call from Patsy or Joe. 'Ray, Frankie is coming. Send two cases of Dom to his mother's house in New Jersey.' I knew Frank's mother, and I always delivered wine to her personally. I still remember at Frank's father's funeral, Frank was escorting his mother down the aisle of the church when she spotted me and my wife. She stopped and whispered something to Frank—I guess she told him who I was—because he stopped and came over and shook my hand and said he was glad to meet me.

"My wife and I and our three sons have been eating at Patsy's since maybe 1955. It's like going home—they're family. It's great food and we always have a good time. One of the funniest things I remember is when I took Primo Carnero to the restaurant—he was the heavyweight champ then, and maybe six foot nine. I introduced Patsy to Primo, and Primo lifted him into the air and gave him a hug.

"You know what makes Patsy's Restaurant so special? Other places, you go in, and they smile, but you know that smile is just business, it doesn't mean anything. The smiles that you get at Patsy's when you walk in—you can tell they really are happy to see you.

"My favorite dishes? I like everything, but I really go for the Roasted Peppers, sometimes with anchovies, and the very special way Sal prepares Chilean sea bass. And of course all those wonderful soups."

ZUCCHINI
AND EGG SOUP

HERE'S ANOTHER USE FOR THAT VERSATILE VEGETABLE ZUCCHINI. THIS
easily prepared soup can be followed successfully by a pasta or chicken dish.

SERVES 8

6 small green zucchini, rinsed

⅓ cup olive oil

2 medium yellow onions, diced

2 extra-large eggs, beaten

¼ cup freshly grated Parmigiano-
 Reggiano

3 tablespoons chopped fresh basil

Salt and freshly ground black pepper,
 to taste

Trim and discard the ends of the zucchini. Halve the zucchini lengthwise, then slice crosswise into ¾-inch half-moons. Reserve.

Heat the oil in a large saucepan or soup pot over medium flame and sauté the onions
about 3 minutes, stirring occasionally, until lightly browned. Add the sliced zucchini and
sauté, stirring, for about 4 minutes, or until zucchini is lightly browned.

Add 6 cups water and bring to a boil. Cover, reduce the heat to low, and simmer for
15 minutes, or until the zucchini is tender.

While the soup is cooking, combine the eggs and Parmigiano-Reggiano in a medium
bowl and mix until thoroughly blended. Whisk the egg mixture into the soup, add the
basil, and simmer for 1 minute. Season with salt and pepper.

Some Pictures from the Old Days

Patsy, circa 1937.

View of Fifty-sixth Street, before Patsy's moved in.

Grandma and my dad in 1951.

Grandma and Grandpa on vacation (LEFT) and in town (BELOW).

My dad (STANDING IN MIDDLE) at the restaurant, age 21.

WE'RE FAMOUS FOR THOSE RED-SAUCE dishes that are making a comeback. These are the same dishes that we've always served, but we made them with respect— pasta favorites like Penne Bolognese, Linguine Napolitano, and my Aunt Anna's favorite: Rigatoni Sorrentino.

I think that the reason these southern-Italian dishes fell out of favor was that they weren't properly prepared. Cheaply made pasta—not the kind we use, which is imported from Italy and made with semolina so it has a texture—was cooked until limp and then dressed with a can of tomato sauce.

But at Patsy's we stayed true to the way my grandfather cooked, following recipes that were handed down from generation to generation, and prepared with care and the best ingredients. We've always been a red-sauce restaurant, that's why people come to us.

"There are so many wonderful things you can do with pasta," says Anna, "including leftover pasta—take a look at my special recipe for a frittata made with pasta from the night before. And about that Rigatoni Sorrentino, a favorite of Jackie Gleason's—it's made with three cheeses and our special sauce. Jackie loved it, and if he didn't have time to come in to the restaurant he would call, and we would send it to his hotel suite."

PASTA, RISOTTO, AND SAUCES

TOMATO SAUCE

FETTUCCINE ALFREDO

FETTUCCINE TOSSED WITH FRESH TOMATOES
AND BASIL

BUCATINI ALL' AMATRICIANA

PENNE BOLOGNESE

LINGUINE WITH ARTICHOKE HEARTS AND OLIVES

PROSCIUTTO AND MELON SAUCE OVER LINGUINE

LINGUINE NAPOLITANO

ORECCHIETTE WITH BROCCOLINI AND SAUSAGE

PENNE WITH ROASTED EGGPLANT

RIGATONI WITH CHICKEN AND MUSHROOMS

FARFALLA PAPALINA

RIGATONI SORRENTINO

TIMBALLO DI MACCHERONI ALLA PATSY'S

SPAGHETTI FRUTTI DI MARE

AUNT ANNA'S GENOVESE SAUCE

PESTO

RISOTTO CON FUNGHI

RISOTTO FRUTTI DI MARE

PREPARING *Pasta*

There's nothing difficult or mysterious about cooking pasta. All you need is a large pot, plenty of water, salt, and a long fork to give the pasta an occasional stir. If you don't want the pasta to stick together, use 4 quarts of water for every pound of pasta.

Bring the water to a rolling boil. Add 1 tablespoon of salt followed by the pasta. You can check the pasta package for cooking time, but we found that it is often excessive. Thin pastas such as spaghetti, linguine, and capellini take less time to cook than larger and heavier shapes such as ziti, penne, or bucatini.

While the pasta cooks, stir it occasionally with a long fork. That stir and the large amount of water will prevent the pasta from sticking together in an unsightly clump.

Cook the pasta until it is just al dente, or firm to the bite. Sample the pasta a few minutes before the cooking time recommended on the package. What you don't want is limp, mushy pasta.

When the pasta is cooked, drain immediately in a large colander and continue with the recipe. If the dish you're preparing calls for sauce, have the sauce prepared before you cook the pasta. The sauce can wait for the pasta, but the pasta cannot wait for the sauce.

TOMATO SAUCE

THIS IS THE SAUCE THAT MY GRANDMOTHER CONCETTA MADE FOR THE entire family when we gathered at my grandparents' house for Monday dinner. Back then, Patsy's Restaurant was closed on Mondays. (Today we're open seven days a week.) Here's my grandmother's version; you'll find many uses for it throughout the book. If your time is limited, a jar of Patsy's sauce is a great alternative.

MAKES 7 CUPS

4½ to 5 pounds ripe plum tomatoes

¼ cup olive oil

1 small yellow onion, minced
   (about ⅓ cup)

3 garlic cloves, quartered

1 ounce Merlot or other dry red wine

2 bay leaves

Salt and freshly ground black pepper,
   to taste

2 tablespoons tomato paste (optional)

¼ cup chopped fresh basil

1 tablespoon chopped fresh flat-leaf
   parsley

Bring a large pot of water to a boil. Remove the stem core from each of the tomatoes, and cut an X on the bottoms. Add the tomatoes to the boiling water and cook for 2 minutes. Drain and allow to cool, then remove the skins, coarsely chop, and set aside.

Heat the oil in a large saucepan over medium flame and sauté the onion and garlic until soft and golden, about 3 minutes. Add the wine and tomatoes (with their juices), increase the heat to high, and bring to a boil. Add the bay leaves, reduce the heat to low, and simmer, covered, for 35 minutes, stirring occasionally. Remove and discard the bay leaves and continue to simmer for 25 minutes. Season with salt and pepper. Stir in the tomato paste (if using) and add the basil and parsley. Simmer uncovered for 5 minutes. Remove and discard the garlic.

FETTUCCINE ALFREDO

"ALFREDO OF ROME CAME TO PATSY'S A FEW YEARS AGO," SAYS ANNA, "and we served him our Fettuccine Alfredo. He said it was better than his. That's because we make it the old-fashioned Neapolitan way, with egg yolks, which really gives this dish a wonderful, rich taste." This dish is best if prepared in a casserole that can be brought from the stove to the table.

SERVES 4

1 pound fettuccine, cooked al dente

2 cups light cream

2 tablespoons unsalted butter

Salt and freshly ground black pepper,
    to taste

½ cup freshly grated Parmigiano-
    Reggiano

2 large egg yolks, lightly beaten

Place the cooked fettuccine in a large casserole that can be heated on top of the stove. Add the cream, butter, and salt and pepper to taste; the liquid should be slightly soupy. Cook, stirring to combine, over very low heat for 3 minutes. Stir in the cheese.

Remove from the heat and quickly stir in the egg yolks. Return to low heat and toss until the pasta is coated, about 1 minute. Serve immediately.

Burton Rocks
"THE DAY I BECAME A LAWYER"

"I first came to Patsy's with my mom and dad, and Hall of Fame baseball announcer Ernie Harwell. We sat upstairs, and felt like part of the family; that's how we feel whenever we come to Patsy's. "It's where we go to celebrate, and that's where we were—my parents and U.S. Open champion Andy North and his wife—when we

FETTUCCINE TOSSED WITH FRESH TOMATOES AND BASIL

IF YOU'RE LOOKING FOR A PERFECT SUMMER MAIN COURSE, THIS IS IT. THE tomato and basil sauce isn't cooked, but is allowed to marinate in olive oil until the flavors are mellow and blended. This is also a wonderful party or buffet dish at any time of the year, because it can be prepared in advance and served at room temperature, with absolutely no last-minute hassles.

SERVES 6

3 large ripe tomatoes, diced (about 4 cups)

½ cup (loosely packed) shredded fresh basil leaves

10 garlic cloves, thinly sliced

⅓ cup plus 2 tablespoons extra-virgin olive oil

Salt and freshly ground black pepper, to taste

1 pound fettuccine, cooked al dente

1 cup grated provolone (about 4 ounces)

In a large bowl, combine the tomatoes, basil, garlic, and ⅓ cup of oil. Season to taste with salt and pepper. Cover and marinate at room temperature for three hours.

To serve, add the cooked fettuccine to the tomato mixture, sprinkle with the cheese and remaining oil, and toss.

celebrated my being admitted to the New York State Bar. That's also where we were on my mother's birthday, enjoying a fabulous Cannoli Cake that Sal had baked especially for my mom.

"Patsy's really knows how to treat their customers. They use the finest ingredients and serve authentic Italian food. I usually eat there twice a month. I have a number of favorite dishes, among them Veal Piccata and Fettuccine Alfredo, and the best sauce of all, Tomato Basil."

BUCATINI ALL' AMATRICIANA

THIS LONG, TUBULAR PASTA ABSORBS THE TASTY SAUCE PERFECTLY. It was originally prepared with pancetta, but I've substituted regular bacon. I think a perfect supper menu is an appetizer of Stuffed Artichokes, followed by Bucatini all' Amatriciana served as a main course.

SERVES 4 TO 6

3 tablespoons olive oil

1 medium yellow onion, finely diced

1 28-ounce can plum tomatoes, with juice

4 slices bacon, diced, cooked crisp, and drained

⅛ pound prosciutto, julienned

2 tablespoons unsalted butter (optional)

Pinch of oregano

2 tablespoons chopped fresh basil

Salt and freshly ground black pepper, to taste

1 pound bucatini pasta, cooked al dente

Heat the olive oil in a large skillet over medium-high flame and sauté the onions for 4 to 5 minutes, or until browned. Coarsely chop the tomatoes and add with juice to the skillet. Bring to a boil, reduce the heat to low, cover, and simmer for 35 minutes.

Add the cooked bacon, prosciutto, butter (if using), and oregano, and simmer for 5 minutes. Stir in the basil, season to taste with salt and pepper, and serve over the cooked bucatini.

PENNE
BOLOGNESE

OUR BOLOGNESE SAUCE IS A GREAT FAVORITE, EVEN THOUGH IT'S PREPARED without the usual cream. It has just enough butter to create the expected smooth texture. And because it contains meat, I think it can be successfully served as a main course following something like an arugula salad. Dessert may be light or rich: Poached Pears make an excellent finale, but no one says no to a Chocolate Mousse.

SERVES 4 TO 6

6 medium white mushrooms, cleaned
   and sliced
¼ cup olive oil
1 small yellow onion, finely chopped
3 garlic cloves, minced
½ pound finely ground lean beef
1 16-ounce can plum tomatoes, with juice
2 bay leaves
¼ cup Cabernet Sauvignon
¼ cup beef broth

Pinch of oregano
2 tablespoons unsalted butter
1 tablespoon chopped fresh flat-leaf
   parsley
Salt and freshly ground black pepper,
   to taste
4 tablespoons freshly grated Parmigiano-
   Reggiano
1 pound penne (or spirali pasta), cooked
   al dente

Bring a large pot of water to a boil, add the mushrooms, and blanch for 2 minutes. Drain, chop fine, and reserve.

Heat the oil in a large skillet over medium-high flame and sauté the onions for 3 to 4 minutes, or until lightly browned. Add the blanched mushrooms, garlic, and ground beef, and continue to cook and stir for 7 to 8 minutes, until the meat is browned. Coarsely chop the tomatoes and add with their juice, the bay leaves, wine, broth, and oregano. Bring to a boil, reduce the heat to low, cover, and simmer for 15 minutes.

Remove the bay leaves. Add the butter and parsley and season with salt and pepper. Sprinkle and stir in the Parmigiano-Reggiano and serve over the cooked pasta.

LINGUINE WITH
ARTICHOKE HEARTS
AND OLIVES

WE USE MANY FRESH ARTICHOKES AT PATSY'S RESTAURANT, BUT WHEN IT comes to a dish that calls for artichoke hearts we buy them prepared, and so should you. Look for jars of artichoke hearts packed in water, and choose those that are light in color. Today there are jars of other interesting vegetables that you might want to keep handy: roasted peppers, onions, eggplant, mushrooms. The ones I think are best are those imported from Italy and packed in oil. They can brighten a relish platter and make a wonderful addition to an antipasto selection.

SERVES 4

¼ cup olive oil

8 garlic cloves, thinly sliced

8 artichoke hearts (canned in water),
   drained and quartered

¼ cup kalamata or gaeta olives, pitted
   and chopped

1¼ cups chicken broth

4 plum tomatoes, coarsely chopped

8 basil leaves

Salt and freshly ground black pepper,
   to taste

1 pound linguine, cooked al dente

2 tablespoons freshly grated Parmigiano-
   Reggiano

Heat the oil in large nonstick skillet over medium flame. Add the garlic and sauté for 1 to 2 minutes, until golden. Add the quartered artichoke hearts, the olives, and the broth and bring to a boil. Reduce the heat to low and allow the liquid to simmer for about 5 minutes, or until reduced by half. Add the tomatoes and basil, and cook an additional 2 to 3 minutes. Season with salt and pepper.

Place the cooked linguine in a serving bowl. Spoon the sauce over the pasta and toss to combine. Sprinkle with grated Parmigiano-Reggiano.

"Debbie Reynolds and I have been friends and associates for over forty years, and we've enjoyed many a meal together at Patsy's. I had my first real Italian meal at Patsy's, and I've never forgotten it—it was lasagna, and I've never had it as good anywhere else."

—MARGIE DUNCAN

Steve Lawrence AND Eydie Gorme

"Eating at Patsy's was not just dinner, but a great experience of friendship and great food," says Steve Lawrence. "One night it was our anniversary and Frank Sinatra, the Chairman of the Board, hosted a dinner for us. Frank got up with a drink in his hand to wish us well, and said, 'May you live to be 102, and may the last voice you hear be mine.'

"Eydie, who had a drink as well, stood up and responded to Frank: 'I never have a martini, just two or three at the most, because two I'm under the table, and three I'm under the host.'

"Frank broke up, hysterically laughing, and threw a meatball at me. I quickly asked for a side order of linguine to go along with it."

PROSCIUTTO
AND MELON SAUCE
OVER LINGUINE

I WAS PREPARING AN APPETIZER OF PROSCIUTTO AND MELON IN THE kitchen when I decided to combine the two ingredients in a pasta sauce. I offered tastes to customers having dinner. They loved it, and one person said that Brillat-Savarin, the eighteenth-century French food writer, said that discovering a new dish creates more pleasure than discovering a star. I don't know about that, but here's a new dish that I hope creates pleasure. Any type of melon may be substituted for Crenshaw. Consider cantaloupe, honeydew, Canary, or a combination of melons for a truly colorful dish.

SERVES 4

1 ripe Crenshaw melon (about 2½ to
   3 pounds)

2 tablespoons butter

8 thin slices prosciutto (about ¼ pound),
   diced

¾ cup Tomato Sauce (page 105)

⅓ cup light cream

2 tablespoons freshly grated Parmigiano-
   Reggiano, plus more for garnish

Salt and freshly ground black pepper,
   to taste

1 pound linguine, cooked al dente

Cut the melon in half and scoop out the seeds. Cut the flesh away from the rind and dice into small pieces.

Heat the butter in a large nonstick skillet over medium flame and sauté the melon and the prosciutto for 3 to 4 minutes, stirring occasionally, until the melon is tender.

Add the tomato sauce, cream, and cheese and stir to combine. Season to taste with salt and pepper. Bring to a boil, reduce the heat to low, cover, and simmer for 1 minute. If the sauce is too thick, thin with water.

Place the cooked linguine in a large serving bowl. Spoon the melon-prosciutto sauce over the pasta and toss to combine. Sprinkle with additional Parmigiano-Reggiano and serve immediately.

LINGUINE NAPOLITANO

THIS IS A DISH WITH STRONG FLAVORS, AND OUR ITALIAN FRIENDS TELL US that it tastes especially good after a late night out, some time like three or four in the morning. I think it tastes delicious at any time, and our customers who order it don't feel they have to wait until after midnight to enjoy it.

SERVES 4

¼ cup olive oil

6 garlic cloves, thinly sliced

1 28-ounce can plum tomatoes, with juice

4 cherry peppers, seeded and chopped

4 anchovy fillets, in oil, drained and
    chopped

2 tablespoons nonpareil capers, rinsed
    and drained

24 green olives, pitted and chopped

3 tablespoons chopped fresh basil

2 tablespoons chopped fresh flat-leaf
    parsley

Freshly ground black pepper, to taste

1 pound linguine, cooked al dente

¼ cup freshly grated Parmigiano-
    Reggiano (optional)

Heat the oil in a large saucepan over low heat and sauté the garlic for 1 to 2 minutes, or until golden. Coarsely chop the tomatoes and add with their juice to the saucepan. Stir in the cherry peppers, anchovies, capers, olives, basil, and parsley. Bring to a boil, reduce the heat to low, cover, and simmer for 25 minutes. Season with black pepper.

Place the cooked linguine in a large serving bowl. Pour the sauce over the pasta and toss to combine. Sprinkle with Parmigiano-Reggiano, if desired, and serve immediately.

ORECCHIETTE
WITH BROCCOLINI AND SAUSAGE

BROCCOLINI IS AN INTERESTING HYBRID VEGETABLE. IT LOOKS LIKE TINY baby broccoli and tastes somewhere between broccoli and asparagus. It needs only a quick rinse before cooking. It is generally sold in half-pound packages and can be prepared with a quick sauté or added to a sauce. Regular broccoli may be substituted.

SERVES 4 TO 6

4 sweet Italian sausages (about 1 pound)

¼ cup olive oil

8 garlic cloves, sliced

1 16-ounce can plum tomatoes, with juice

1 medium red bell pepper, cut into ½-inch strips

1 pound broccolini

¼ cup chopped fresh basil

Salt and freshly ground black pepper, to taste

1 pound orecchiette, cooked al dente

Preheat the broiler.

Prick the sausages all over with a fork, place in a nonstick pan, and broil, turning to brown on all sides, until cooked through, about 15 minutes. Remove from broiler, slice thin, and reserve.

Heat the oil in a Dutch oven or large skillet over medium flame. Add the garlic and sauté for 1 to 2 minutes, or until lightly browned. Coarsely chop the tomatoes and add with their juice to the skillet. Bring to a boil, cover, and cook for 20 minutes. Add the red bell pepper, broccolini, and ¼ cup water. Cook over medium heat, stirring occasionally, until broccolini is just crisp-tender, about 4 minutes.

Add the basil, reserved sausages, and 1 cup of water, and bring to a simmer. Season with salt and pepper and cook for 5 minutes, until heated through.

Place the cooked orecchiette in a large serving bowl. Spoon the sauce over the pasta and toss to combine.

PENNE WITH
ROASTED EGGPLANT

ROASTING A VEGETABLE SUCH AS EGGPLANT MELLOWS THE TASTE, AND IN this recipe makes a perfect foil to the stronger flavors of the capers, olives, and anchovies.

SERVES 4

2 medium Italian eggplants (about
  ½ pound)

6 tablespoons olive oil

½ teaspoon salt

¼ teaspoon freshly ground black pepper,
  plus more to taste

3 cloves garlic, thinly sliced

1 16-ounce can plum tomatoes, with juice

1 anchovy fillet in oil, drained and
  chopped

2 tablespoons nonpareil capers, rinsed
  and drained

¼ cup pitted and chopped gaeta or
  kalamata olives

1 pound penne, cooked al dente

¼ cup freshly grated Parmigiano-
  Reggiano

Preheat the oven to 450°F.

Wash the eggplants, trim the ends (don't peel), and cut into small cubes.

Coat the bottom of a baking dish with 1 tablespoon of the oil. Place the eggplant cubes in the dish and spoon over 2 tablespoons oil. Season with the salt and pepper and roast in the preheated oven for 10 to 14 minutes, turning every 5 minutes, until lightly browned and tender.

Meanwhile, heat the remaining 3 tablespoons of oil in a large saucepan over medium flame. Add the garlic and sauté for 1 to 2 minutes, or until lightly golden. Add the tomatoes with their juice. Bring to a boil, reduce the heat to low, and simmer, covered, for 25 minutes. Add the anchovy, capers, and olives and bring to a boil. Reduce the heat to low, add the eggplant, cover, and simmer for 5 to 7 minutes, or until heated through. Season to taste with additional pepper.

Place the cooked penne in a serving dish. Spoon the sauce over the pasta, toss to combine, and sprinkle with Parmigiano-Reggiano.

RIGATONI
WITH CHICKEN AND MUSHROOMS

HERE'S A WONDERFUL COMBINATION OF PASTA AND CHICKEN. I THINK OF it as a truly hunter's-style dish—I can picture it being served after a day out in the open. In my imagination, I see the hunter as a benign person, or maybe just a terrible shot, so rather than bringing a rabbit home for the pot, he'll enjoy a chicken that was raised to be eaten. This is one of Rush Limbaugh's favorites.

SERVES 4 TO 6

¾ pound white mushrooms, cleaned and thinly sliced

½ cup all-purpose flour

2 boneless and skinless chicken breasts (about 1 pound), split and rinsed

½ cup olive oil

1 medium yellow onion, diced

2 cups canned Italian plum tomatoes, with juice

1 cup chicken broth

¼ cup dry white wine

¼ cup sweet Marsala

1 tablespoon butter

2 tablespoons chopped flat-leaf parsley

Salt and freshly ground black pepper, to taste

1 pound rigatoni, cooked al dente

Bring a large pot of water to a boil. Add the mushrooms and blanch for 2 minutes. Drain and reserve.

Spread the flour on a large plate. Dip the chicken breasts in the flour and lightly coat. Heat the oil in a large nonstick skillet over medium-high flame and sauté the chicken until lightly browned on both sides, about 6 minutes. Remove from the skillet, allow to cool, and cut into bite-size pieces. Reserve.

Add the onions to the skillet and sauté over medium heat for about 3 minutes, stirring occasionally, until the onions are just lightly browned. Coarsely chop the tomatoes and add with their juice; bring to a boil. Cover, reduce the heat to low, and simmer for 10 to 12 minutes, or until all ingredients are heated through and blended.

Return the cooked chicken to the skillet and add the reserved mushrooms, broth, wine, Marsala, butter, and parsley. Cover and simmer for 10 minutes, or until all ingredients are heated through. Season with salt and pepper.

Place the cooked rigatoni in a large serving bowl. Spoon the chicken and sauce over the pasta and toss to combine.

Meredith Vieira

"My husband Richard's great-uncle Murray introduced us to Patsy's," says Meredith Vieira, moderator of *The View*. "Patsy and Murray had become friends in the thirties when Patsy was just a busboy with big dreams of one day opening his own restaurant. Well, he got his wish. But along the way he never forgot his friend. Every morning the two of them would share breakfast together. Even after Patsy died, Murray continued their daily ritual: He would walk over to the restaurant before it opened and rap on the windows with his cane. Patsy's son, Joe, was always waiting with a hot cup of coffee and Italian pastries for his dad's old friend. That's Patsy's to me—not just a place to eat, but family. And the food ain't bad, either.

"My favorite dishes? If I can have Patsy's Chopped Salad followed by their Eggplant Parmigiana and finish the meal with cannolis I feel as though I've died and gone to heaven. . . . Better yet, I've gone to Patsy's."

FARFALLA PAPALINA

A RECIPE MADE TO PLEASE A POPE, THIS IS A VERSION OF THE MORE familiar carbonara sauce. It's an extremely rich sauce with an almost soupy consistency. I suggest a light starter and dessert.

SERVES 6 TO 8

6 large white mushrooms, cleaned and
    thinly sliced

2 tablespoons olive oil

3 cups light cream

2 tablespoons unsalted butter

1 10-ounce package frozen peas, cooked

¼ pound prosciutto, julienned

1 tablespoon chopped fresh flat-leaf
    parsley

1 pound farfalla pasta, cooked al dente

4 tablespoons freshly grated Parmigiano-
    Reggiano

Salt and freshly ground black pepper,
    to taste

3 large egg yolks

Bring a medium pot of water to a boil, add the mushrooms, and blanch for 2 minutes. Drain and reserve.

Heat the oil in a large saucepan over medium flame and sauté the blanched mushrooms for 3 to 4 minutes, or until browned. Drain any excess oil. Add the cream, butter, peas, prosciutto, parsley, and cooked pasta, and bring to a boil. Stir in the Parmigiano-Reggiano, and season with salt and pepper.

Remove the pan from the heat and quickly stir in the egg yolks. Return to low heat, toss until the pasta is coated with all ingredients, and cook for 2 to 3 minutes, or until heated through. The consistency will be that of thick soup. Serve immediately.

RIGATONI
SORRENTINO

"THIS IS ABSOLUTELY ONE OF MY FAVORITE DISHES," SAYS ANNA, "AND IT was a favorite of Jackie Gleason's too. When he didn't have the time to come to Patsy's, we would have this dish delivered to his hotel suite. I think it's the use of three cheeses that makes it so delicious."

SERVES 6 TO 8

4 cups Tomato Sauce (page 105)
½ pound fresh ricotta cheese
1 pound rigatoni, cooked al dente

2 cups shredded mozzarella (about 1 pound)
1½ cups freshly grated Parmigiano-Reggiano

Preheat the broiler.

In a large saucepan, bring the sauce to a boil. Remove from the heat, pour half the sauce into a bowl, and reserve.

Add the ricotta and the cooked rigatoni to the saucepan with the sauce, mix to combine, and bring to a simmer over low heat.

Spoon the hot rigatoni-sauce mixture into a baking dish and add the reserved sauce. Top with the shredded mozzarella and grated Parmigiano-Reggiano and broil until the cheeses have melted, about 6 to 8 minutes. Serve immediately.

Jaclyn Smith

"I started going to Patsy's when my kids were very young. There wasn't anything that the Scognamillos would not do for them. My kids are grown, but it's still my first choice when I'm in New York. I'm always welcome like one of the family, and the food makes me feel like one of the family. I love the Chopped Salad and the Rigatoni Sorrentino."

TIMBALLO
DI MACCHERONI ALLA PATSY'S

MANY OF OUR CUSTOMERS SAW THE FILM *BIG NIGHT,* WHICH TOOK PLACE in an Italian restaurant. The highlight of the movie was a timballo—a drum-shaped vegetable mold filled with a pasta mixture, served at a very special banquet. It was so impressive that many people asked if I had seen the movie and if I could prepare the dish.

Not only can I prepare a timballo, but my grandfather served it fifty years ago at our restaurant. From time to time I've had a timballo on our menu, and because so many customers requested it, I've created a version to be prepared at home. This timballo is baked in a 10-inch springform pan for easier serving. I've cut the recipe down to serve 12 to 14—it's a perfect party dish, and makes quite an impression on a buffet table.

SERVES 12 TO 14

2 to 3 large eggplants (about 3 pounds), ends trimmed

¾ cup all-purpose flour

4 large eggs, lightly beaten

½ cup olive oil

1 teaspoon salt

¼ teaspoon freshly ground black pepper

1¼ pounds penne, cooked al dente

1 10-ounce package frozen green peas, thawed

½ cup plus 2 tablespoons freshly grated Parmigiano-Reggiano

½ cup plus 2 tablespoons freshly grated provolone

8 ounces mozzarella, cubed

¼ cup chopped fresh basil

¼ cup chopped fresh flat-leaf parsley

8 cups Tomato Sauce (page 105)

1 tablespoon butter

½ cup dry bread crumbs

6 hard-boiled eggs, peeled and cut in half

Preheat the oven to 375°F.

Peel the eggplants, halve lengthwise, and cut each half into thin slices, about $1/8$ inch thick (a mandoline or meat slicer can ensure uniform slices). Spread the flour on a large plate. Coat each eggplant slice in the flour, and then dip in the beaten egg.

Heat the oil in a large nonstick skillet over medium flame and sauté the eggplant slices in batches until lightly browned on both sides, about 5 minutes. Using a slotted spatula, remove the slices from the skillet and place on paper towels to drain. Season with 1 teaspoon of the salt and $1/2$ teaspoon of the pepper. Set aside.

In a large bowl combine the cooked penne, peas, Parmigiano-Reggiano, provolone, mozzarella, basil, parsley, and $4^{1/2}$ cups of the sauce. Mix thoroughly.

Butter the insides and bottom of a 10-inch springform pan and coat with the bread crumbs.

Divide the eggplant slices into 2 parts. Working from the center of the pan, drape half the eggplant slices over the edge of the pan. Cover the bottom of the pan with half the remaining eggplant slices. Season with the remaining salt and pepper. Spoon the pasta mixture into the center of the pan. Place the hard-boiled cooked eggs along the inside edge of the pan, pressing gently into the pasta mixture. Place the remaining eggplant slices on top of the pasta, bring the ends of the draped eggplant over the top of the mixture, and cover with $1/2$ cup of sauce.

Cover the timballo with aluminum foil and bake in the preheated oven for 1 hour. Allow to cool and refrigerate for at least 3 hours before removing the sides of springform pan. Cut into slices and serve. (You may want to show your guests the timballo before cutting it into individual slices.) Heat the remaining 3 cups of sauce and spoon onto plates. Place a timballo slice over sauce.

Anna, JACKIE KENNEDY, MEL TORMÉ, AND SEAN "PUFFY" COMBS

"I think my mother is one of the most popular members of our family," says Frank DiCola, Anna's son. "She says exactly what's on her mind, and most people love her for it.

"Some years back, Jackie Kennedy Onassis came to dinner with her son, John, who was about seventeen at the time. John didn't have a jacket, and my mother said she would give him one of the house jackets to wear. I think Mrs. Kennedy Onassis was taken aback. 'You're going to make my son wear a jacket?' she asked. But my mother was firm. 'It's the policy of the house,' she said, and sure enough John put on one of our jackets.

"We no longer require jackets; times are more casual—and John Kennedy Jr. came here many times for lunch when he was editor of *George* magazine, wearing a windbreaker jacket and a baseball cap worn backward. He didn't hold that house jacket against us. He was a great presence, and we all miss him.

"And then there was Mel Tormé. My mother was talking to him, and Mel realized that she didn't know who he was or what he did. 'I'm known as the Velvet Fog,' he said, trying to get my mother to recognize his importance as a singer.

"'Of course,' my mother said, polite but unaware of his fame. Later, when Sal came in, she said, 'You know who was here for lunch? The Velvet Frog.'

"And then there was the time Don Ameche, the famous movie star, came to dinner, and my mother looked at him and said, 'I can't remember whether you invented the telephone or the telegraph.'

"But I think one of my favorite Anna stories was when Sean Combs (aka Puff Daddy) came here for lunch. I told my mother who he was, his nickname, and how much my son loved his music.

"'Really?' my mother said. 'You think it would be okay if I asked for his autograph?'

"Sean Combs is a friendly guy—I've seen other diners ask for his autograph, and he always obliges with a smile, even when they're interrupting his meal, so I told my mother to go ahead.

"And what does she say? She goes over to Sean Combs and says, "Excuse me, Mr. Daddy. I would like your autograph for my grandchildren. They really like your music. Me, I don't listen to that crazy music. I listen to Frank Sinatra and Tony Bennett.'

"Sean Combs laughed and wrote a couple of sentences to my son, who was thrilled, of course.

"Even though we have a wide variety of dishes on our menus, sometimes my mother comes in with a dish she's prepared at home—her Sauce Genovese, for instance. The family and staff enjoy it for lunch, and then my mother presents tastings to some of our customers. To her, Patsy's is an extension of her home."

SPAGHETTI FRUTTI DI MARE

PASTA AND SEAFOOD MAKE A GREAT COMBINATION. THIS RECIPE CALLS for quite an assortment, but you can adapt it to your preference. If you don't care for calamari, for example, you can substitute additional shrimp or clams. For a spicier version of this dish, add 1 teaspoon of crushed red pepper flakes.

SERVES 4 TO 6

3 tablespoons olive oil

3 cloves garlic, minced

1 28-ounce can plum tomatoes, with juice

¼ cup dry white wine

½ pound cleaned calamari, cut into
  ½-inch rings

½ pound small shrimp, cleaned and
  halved

16 littleneck clams, scrubbed

16 mussels, cleaned (see headnote on
  page 51)

¼ cup chopped fresh basil

¼ cup chopped fresh flat-leaf parsley

Salt and freshly ground black pepper,
  to taste

1 pound spaghetti, cooked al dente

In a large saucepan, heat the oil over a medium flame. Add the garlic and sauté for 1 to 2 minutes, until soft and golden. Coarsely chop the tomatoes and add with their juice to the saucepan. Add the wine and the calamari and bring to a boil. Lower the heat, cover, and simmer for 25 to 28 minutes, or until calamari is tender.

Raise the heat to medium and add the shrimp, clams, and mussels to the sauce. Cook covered for about 10 minutes, or until the clam and mussel shells open; discard any that don't. Stir in the basil and parsley and cook for an additional 2 minutes. Season with salt and pepper.

Place the cooked spaghetti in a serving bowl. Spoon the sauce and seafood over the pasta and toss to combine.

AUNT ANNA'S
GENOVESE SAUCE

"WHEN MY PARENTS CAME TO THE UNITED STATES FROM NAPLES IN 1923," says Anna, "they had very little money. That was true of most of the people who came from southern Italy at that time. And most of them had big families. They really had to stretch food—make it go a long way. This sauce is an example of how they did it.

"The meat that's in the sauce is a piece of chuck, not tender, like sirloin, but very flavorful, and inexpensive. It's a sauce you make while you're at home and doing other things. You let the sauce cook for hours until the meat just about dissolves, and then you puree the whole thing and serve it with pasta. It's real home-style cooking, satisfying and full of flavor. My mother made it often and so do I—all the kids love it. I prefer it with fresh fettuccine."

MAKES 3 CUPS

¼ cup olive oil

½ pound beef chuck, cubed

1 large yellow onion, chopped

4 ribs celery, chopped

2 large carrots, sliced

¼ cup dry white wine

½ cup chopped fresh basil

¼ teaspoon ground nutmeg

2 tablespoons butter

Salt and freshly ground black pepper,
   to taste

Heat the oil in a large Dutch oven over medium flame and sauté the beef for about 5 minutes, stirring occasionally, until browned. Remove and reserve.

Lower the heat, add the onion, celery, and carrots, and sauté for 5 to 6 minutes, or until the onions are lightly browned. Return the meat to the pot and add the wine and water to cover. Stir to combine and bring to a boil. Reduce the heat to low, cover, and cook for 1 to 1½ hours, adding water as necessary, until the meat is tender and falls into shreds.

Stir in the basil, nutmeg, and butter, and cook for an additional 5 minutes. Season with salt and pepper.

Transfer the sauce to a food processor or blender and purée, adding water if the sauce is too thick. Return the purée to the Dutch oven and heat over medium flame until warmed through. Serve over pasta.

THANKSGIVING FOR *Rush Limbaugh*

"That Thanksgiving Day dinner for Frank Sinatra," says Joe, "reminds me of a Thanksgiving dinner that Sal and Frank and I prepared for Rush Limbaugh. It was just a couple of years ago, when Rush had his TV show here in New York, and he called on a Tuesday or maybe Wednesday just before Thanksgiving and asked if the restaurant would be open on Thanksgiving. I told him that we always closed on Thanksgiving, and Rush said, 'What am I going to do? I'm having some people over and I thought I'd bring them to Patsy's.

"'The restaurant is closed,' I told Rush, 'but Sal and Frank and I will come in and make your Thanksgiving dinner, and you can send someone to pick it up.'

"'I'm absolutely not going to let you guys do that,' Rush said. 'Forget it. You're not going to open the restaurant just for me. Don't even think about it.'

"'We won't open the restaurant at all,' I told him, 'just the kitchen, and the three of us will make you the best Thanksgiving dinner you ever had. Now, how many people are you expecting?'

"'No way,' Rush said, 'stay home with your family. Forget about it.'

"'We're going to do it,' I said, 'and if you don't send anyone over to pick it up, it'll be a terrible waste of a great meal.'

"There was nothing much Rush could say after that, and on Thanksgiving Day we opened the restaurant kitchen first thing in the morning and prepared a Thanksgiving dinner, the whole thing—oysters on the half shell, soup, salad, vegetables, big bowl of mashed potatoes, baked sweet potatoes, a turkey with stuffing, and a couple of pies. And Rush sent his driver for it."

Anna continues, "Anyway, Rush Limbaugh had his Thanksgiving dinner. And during his final television show, he said, 'This show is dedicated to Joe Scognamillo of Patsy's Restaurant.' Oh, and you want to know what we had for Thanksgiving? We made turkey for the kids—they hear so much about that at school. As for the rest of us, as I remember we had my Sauce Genovese with pasta, a family favorite."

PESTO

PESTO CAN BE MADE IN A FEW MINUTES IN A FOOD PROCESSOR. SERVE OVER your favorite pasta, adding 2 tablespoons of the hot water in which the pasta has cooked to the sauce. Pesto can also be prepared in advance and frozen for later use. Here at Patsy's we serve it over linguine—cooked al dente, of course.

MAKES 1 CUP

2 firmly packed cups fresh basil leaves (rinsed and drained)

⅔ cup olive oil

2 tablespoons pignoli (pine) nuts

3 garlic cloves, halved

1 teaspoon salt

½ cup freshly grated Parmigiano-Reggiano

Place the basil, oil, nuts, garlic, and salt in food processor and purée thoroughly. Add the cheese and continue processing until all ingredients are completely blended.

Transfer the pesto to a bowl and add 2 tablespoons of hot water from the pasta before serving.

SAUCY *Phyllis Diller*

"Patsy's has always been successful because of the great Italian food with all those authentic flavors you can't fake. Then add the wonderful ambiance and the professional waiters, the great service. My favorite dish is the plain old Spaghetti and Meatballs. I recently discovered they sell their sauces in Los Angeles, so I now come home with jars of Patsy's sauce to keep me happy till I get back to New York."

Anna's Frittata
WITH LEFTOVER PASTA

Sometimes it's hard to know how much pasta to prepare. We recommend one pound of pasta for four people, but depending on what else you're serving and the appetites of guests, you just might end up with leftover cooked pasta.

Don't throw out the leftovers! Anna says, "When I'm preparing pasta for the family, my kids always tell me to make extra so that they can have a pasta frittata the next day. It's delicious, and it doesn't matter what kind of sauce you have on the original dish.

"This works best with spaghetti, linguine, fettuccine, or capellini —the long thin pastas. Let's say you have about 2 cups of leftover pasta with sauce, or maybe just with butter and cheese. Get out an individual omelet or crepe pan—nonstick is best. Heat a little oil or butter in the pan. Combine the cooked pasta with beaten eggs— figure on two eggs per person. Spoon ¼ of the egg-pasta mixture into the crepe pan over low heat. You may want to add some Parmigiano-Reggiano.

"Cook it the way you'd cook any omelet—we call it a frittata. Lift the edges of the omelet and let the eggs flow to the bottom of the pan. Don't cook it too long, just until the eggs set. Keep going with the rest of the pasta-egg mixture—you'll have four frittatas and four happy people.

"If you prefer, you can make one large frittata in a 9- or 10-inch nonstick skillet. Prepare it the same way, and then cut into wedges to serve."

RISOTTO CON FUNGHI

RISOTTO IS THE DELICIOUS ITALIAN WAY OF COOKING RICE AND MAY BE served as a side dish, an appetizer, or as a main course at lunch. The idea is to allow the rice to absorb hot liquid slowly, so the rice swells and acquires a unique consistency: both tender and firm. A wide variety of ingredients can be added to a risotto: vegetables, shellfish, chicken livers, cheese. Risotto is best made with the short-grained Italian rice Arborio. Risotto con Funghi, a Neapolitan favorite, can be prepared with the familiar white mushrooms or with a combination of wild and cultivated mushrooms.

SERVES 4

1 cup dried imported porcini mushrooms
    (about 2 ounces)
¾ pound white mushrooms, cleaned and
    thinly sliced
5 cups chicken broth
¼ cup olive oil
1 large yellow onion, finely chopped
    (about ¾ cup)
1½ cups Arborio rice

¼ cup dry Marsala wine
2 tablespoons butter
¼ cup light cream
¼ cup chopped fresh flat-leaf parsley
¼ cup chopped fresh basil
½ cup freshly grated Parmigiano-
    Reggiano, plus more for garnish
Salt and freshly ground black pepper,
    to taste

In a medium bowl, soak the dried mushrooms in hot water for 20 minutes. After the water turns brown, drain and repeat. The mushrooms should be soaked until all soil particles are removed, usually two changes of water. Drain and reserve. Meanwhile, bring a large pot of water to a boil and blanch the fresh mushroom slices for 2 minutes. Drain and reserve.

In a large saucepan, heat the broth to a simmer, and keep warm over very low flame.

Heat the oil in a large heavy saucepan or casserole over medium flame and sauté the onion until just translucent, about 4 minutes. Add the raw rice and cook, stirring for

1 or 2 minutes, or until rice is coated with oil. Reduce the heat to low and add the Marsala and ¾ cup of the hot broth. When the liquid has been absorbed, add another ¾ cup of broth. Continue adding liquid, letting the rice absorb the broth a little at a time. Stir frequently to prevent sticking. After the rice has cooked for 10 minutes, stir in the reconstituted porcinis and the blanched mushrooms.

When the rice is nearly cooked—tender but still slightly firm to the bite—stir in the butter, cream, parsley, and basil and cook for 2 minutes. The total cooking time of the rice should be 19 to 21 minutes.

Remove from the heat, stir in the grated cheese, and season with salt and pepper. Serve with additional grated cheese on the side.

Mrs. Sinatra
AND HER HOME AWAY FROM HOME

"To us, Patsy's was a home away from home," says Nancy Sinatra Sr. "When I'd come to New York with Frank and the kids, we'd get off the plane, get into a limo, and head straight for Patsy's. Everyone is so nice there, and the food is so good.

"I can't say what dishes I like best, because I like a little bit of everything. Among my favorites, though, is the Fra Diavolo Sauce, which I buy all the time. Anything with that sauce tastes good to me. I don't get in to New York as much as I used to, but when I do come in I go to Patsy's, and my kids go there whenever they're in New York."

RISOTTO FRUTTI DI MARE

THE ITALIAN WAY OF PREPARING RICE IS VERY SPECIAL—THE SLOW COOKING, allowing each grain of rice to absorb the cooking liquid, gives the rice a wonderful, creamy texture. Prepared with seafood, risotto transforms from a side dish to a very special main course. Be sure not to overcook the seafood.

SERVES 4

THE SAUCE

2 tablespoons olive oil

3 cloves garlic, minced

1 16-ounce can whole plum tomatoes,
    with juice

¼ cup dry white wine

½ pound cleaned calamari, cut into
    ½-inch rings

½ pound small shrimp, cleaned and
    halved

16 littleneck clams, scrubbed

16 mussels, cleaned (see page 51)

¼ cup chopped fresh basil

¼ cup chopped fresh flat-leaf parsley

Salt and freshly ground black pepper,
    to taste

THE RISOTTO

5 cups chicken broth

¼ cup olive oil

1 large yellow onion, finely chopped

1½ cups Arborio rice

½ cup freshly grated Parmigiano-
    Reggiano, plus more for garnish

To make the sauce, heat the oil in a large saucepan over medium flame. Add the garlic and sauté for 1 to 2 minutes, until soft and golden. Coarsely chop the tomatoes and add with their juice to the saucepan. Bring to a boil, reduce the heat to low, cover, and simmer for 15 minutes. Add the wine and the calamari and bring to a boil. Reduce the heat to low, cover, and simmer for 22 to 25 minutes, or until the calamari is tender.

Raise the heat to medium and add the shrimp, clams, and mussels. Cook covered for about 10 minutes, or until the clam and mussel shells open (discard those that have not opened). Stir in the basil and parsley and cook for an additional 2 minutes. Season with the salt and pepper. Remove from heat and reserve.

To make the risotto, heat the broth to a simmer in a large saucepan, and keep warm over very low flame.

Heat the oil in a large saucepan over medium flame and sauté the onions for 4 minutes, or until just translucent. Add the raw rice and cook, stirring, for 1 or 2 minutes, until the rice is coated with oil. Reduce the heat to low and add ¾ cup of the hot broth. When the liquid has been absorbed, add another ¾ cup of broth. Continue adding liquid, letting the rice absorb the broth a little at a time. Stir frequently to prevent sticking. The total cooking time of the rice should be 19 to 21 minutes.

When the rice is nearly cooked—tender, but still slightly firm to the bite—stir in the seafood sauce, and remove from the heat. Stir in the Parmigiano-Reggiano, and season with salt and pepper. Serve with additional grated cheese on the side.

Bill Boggs's CORNER TABLE

"I've been going to Patsy's for thirty years. I love to take people there—it's so comfortable it's like being at home. I used to live on the East Side of New York and I would take a cab to Patsy's, no problem. But now I live on the West Side and I can walk to the restaurant. And I do, often.

"To me, Patsy's is like your favorite neighborhood restaurant—the one that had a checkered tablecloth and a candle in a Chianti bottle. You know, the kind of restaurant you would go to as a kid, maybe on a first date. But now, this neighborhood restaurant got all dressed up, went to the big city, and became a *star.* That's Patsy's, a real star.

"One of the first times I went there I saw Frank Sinatra at another table. That told me a lot, and I figured if it was good enough for Frank, it was good enough for me. What are my favorite dishes? I love the Tricolor Salad, and just about any dish as long as it is made with Patsy's Vodka Sauce."

WE HAVE A LOT OF CHICKEN DISHES ON OUR MENU. I recommend chicken to people cooking at home because while some people won't eat fish, and others say no to meat, most people enjoy chicken.

When purchasing chicken, it's important to know your butcher. The fresher the chicken, the better it will taste. Avoid frozen, or even semi-frozen chicken, sometimes called chilled. A free-range chicken is often more flavorful than those cooped-up birds that were never allowed outdoors. It's very important to wash chicken thoroughly and to clean all utensils and cutting boards that have come in contact with the bird. Cook all chicken until well-done—170 degrees internal temperature. You can test by piercing the chicken with a sharp knife; the juices should always run clear. Even the tiniest sign of red means the chicken is not cooked through. You may enjoy a rare steak, but never eat a rare or even medium-rare chicken. Many of our recipes call for boneless breast of chicken, which can be quickly prepared and takes only minutes to reach the well-done state.

CHICKEN

CHICKEN CARDINALE

SPICY LEMON CHICKEN

CHICKEN PARMIGIANA

CHICKEN PICCATA

CHICKEN WITH MUSHROOMS
AND RED PEPPERS

CHICKEN PORTOBELLO

SCALOPPINE DI POLLO ZINGARA

ROLLATINI DI PETTO DI POLLO E SPINACI

HERB-ROASTED CHICKEN

CHICKEN LIVERS WITH PEPPERS

CHICKEN VENEZIANA

CHICKEN CARDINALE

A CARDINAL'S ROBES ARE RED, AS IS THE PLUMAGE OF THE CARDINAL BIRD.
Was this recipe orignally named for one or the other? I don't know, but the red of the
roasted pepper clearly inspired the name.

SERVES 4

8 chicken cutlets (about 1½ to 2 pounds),
    pounded thin

½ teaspoon salt

½ teaspoon freshly ground black pepper

½ cup all-purpose flour

⅓ cup olive oil

¾ cup chicken broth

¼ cup sweet Marsala wine

1 tablespoon unsalted butter

¼ cup chopped fresh flat-leaf parsley

2 Roasted Red Bell Peppers (page 52),
    quartered

8 (2 x 4-inch) slices mozzarella (about
    ¼ pound)

¼ cup freshly grated Parmigiano-
    Reggiano

½ teaspoon cornstarch

Preheat the broiler.

Rinse the chicken, pat dry, season with the salt and pepper, and coat lightly with the
flour. Heat the oil in a large nonstick skillet over medium flame and sauté the chicken
for about 6 minutes, turning once, or until lightly browned on both sides. Drain the oil
from the skillet and discard. Add the broth, wine, butter, and parsley. Cover and simmer over low heat until the chicken is cooked through, about 8 minutes.

Remove the chicken from the skillet to a nonstick broiler pan, leaving the liquid in
the skillet. Place a piece of roasted pepper on each piece of chicken and top with a slice
of mozzarella. Sprinkle with the Parmigiano-Reggiano cheese. Broil until the mozzarella
has melted, about 3 minutes. Remove the chicken from the broiler and place on a serving platter. Keep warm.

Mix the cornstarch with ¼ cup water and whisk it into the skillet. Bring to a simmer over medium heat and cook until the sauce has thickened, about 2 minutes. Adjust the seasoning, spoon over chicken, and serve.

"GET OUT, *Aristotle Onassis!*"

"Patsy's Restaurant," says Joe, "keeps really long hours. We open at twelve noon, and we stay open until ten-thirty—Fridays and Saturdays until eleven-thirty. That's a long day. And you can come into our restaurant at any time between those hours and we'll be happy to serve you. We don't say 'Sorry, we're closed' to someone who comes in at three or four in the afternoon. If that's when they want to eat, that's when they can eat.

"But when it's eleven o'clock at night, we really want to close. We don't put anyone out who's eating dinner—none of that cleaning off the tables and setting up for the next day that I've seen other restaurants do. But we try to keep that front door closed.

"Once, after a very busy day, I was trying to explain all this to a kid I had in the coat-check room. He was from Italy, kind of flighty, and not too swift. I kept explaining to him that when it was eleven o'clock I wanted that front door locked—*locked*. He looked so blank that I could see that he didn't get the message, so to make my point, I said, 'Look, I don't care who comes to the door after eleven. That door stays locked, and you don't let anyone in—I don't care if it's Aristotle Onassis!' Onassis was well known at that time, and the kid finally looked as though he understood.

"So what happens? About eleven-fifteen there's a knocking on the front door, and then there's a banging, and I'm in the back of the restaurant, and I watch the kid go to the door. 'We're closed,' he says. But that doesn't stop the people who want to come in—they keep knocking and banging on the door.

"The kid had learned his lesson, and he says again, 'We're closed!' Then I hear a voice from the other side of the door say, 'I'm Aristotle Onassis.' And the kid yells out, 'My boss says no one gets in. Especially you!'

"I don't think I ever moved so fast in my life. I pushed the kid away and got the door open for Aristotle Onassis, who was with Johnny Meyer, then head of Olympic Airways.

"Ari Onassis looked amused, but Johnny Meyer, a real tough character, said, 'Joe, what the hell is going on?'

"'I'll explain later.' I said. 'Come on in. Now, what can I get you to eat?'"

SPICY
LEMON CHICKEN

HERE'S A GREAT WAY TO PREPARE A SPICY CHICKEN. THIS DISH RELIES ON lemon juice and two kinds of pepper to create a piquant flavor.

SERVES 4

1 chicken (about 3 to 3½ pounds),
    cut into 8 pieces
½ cup fresh lemon juice (from about
    3 lemons)
¼ cup olive oil

1 teaspoon crushed red pepper flakes
1 teaspoon coarsely ground fresh white
    pepper
1 teaspoon salt

Rinse the chicken pieces, pat dry, and place in a deep pan.

In a medium bowl, whisk together the lemon juice, olive oil, red pepper flakes, and white pepper. Mix well. Set aside and refrigerate ¼ cup of the mixture, and pour the remainder over the chicken.

Place the chicken in the refrigerator and marinate for 3 hours, turning pieces every half hour.

Preheat the oven to 400°F.

Remove the chicken from the marinade, discard the marinade, season the chicken with salt, place in a roasting pan, and roast, turning to brown on all sides. Spoon the reserved ¼ cup of lemon juice mixture over the chicken as it roasts. Test for doneness by piercing with a knife; chicken will be done when juices run clear and dark meat is tender, about an hour.

CHICKEN
PARMIGIANA

IF YOU DON'T CARE FOR VEAL, OR FIND IT TOO EXPENSIVE, HERE'S THE perfect substitute: This beloved favorite is prepared with chicken cutlets, rather than veal scaloppine. I have found that many of our customers prefer chicken to veal, and this dish retains all the flavors of the original Parmigiana recipe and loses nothing when prepared with chicken.

SERVES 4

½ cup all-purpose flour

2 large eggs, beaten

¾ cup Seasoned Bread Crumbs
    (page 49)

4 chicken cutlets (about 1 pound),
    pounded thin

¼ cup olive oil

2 cups Tomato Sauce (page 105)

½ pound mozzarella, cubed

3 tablespoons freshly grated Parmigiano-
    Reggiano

Preheat the oven to 400°F.

Spread the flour on a large plate, place the eggs in a shallow bowl, and spread the bread crumbs on a second large plate. Coat each chicken cutlet in the flour, then the beaten eggs, and then the bread crumbs, patting with the palm of your hand to ensure adhesion.

Pour the oil in a 13 × 10 × 2-inch baking dish, add the cutlets, and turn them several times so that both sides are coated with the oil. Bake in the oven for 10 to 12 minutes, turn the cutlets, and continue to bake for an additional 8 minutes.

Remove the dish from the oven, and pour the tomato sauce over the chicken. Spread the sauce smooth with a spatula, and top evenly with the mozzarella. Sprinkle with the Parmigiano-Reggiano and bake for 14 to16 minutes, or until all the ingredients are heated through and the cheese has browned.

Joe Bologna
AND Renee Taylor

"Renee and I spent much of our courtship at Patsy's. It was where we became engaged, and where I put the ring on her finger. That was a memorable time—so memorable that I even remember what we had for dinner: I ate Lobster Fra Diavolo and Renée had Chicken Piccata.

"We go to Patsy's whenever we're in New York. It's the best southern-Italian restaurant in New York, and the family and staff are friendly and create a great ambiance.

"We take Patsy's bottled sauces home with us. We love them, especially the marinara, which tastes just like the sauce Joe's mother used to make—she was the best. Her sauce tasted better every time we ate it, and so does Patsy's.

"Patsy's is also where we go to celebrate. Last year we had an opening-night party at Patsy's when we starred in the Broadway play *If You Ever Leave Me I'm Going with You.* Everyone had a great time. Our good friends Joan Collins and Michele Lee were there."

CHICKEN PICCATA

OUR CUSTOMERS ORDER THIS DISH WHEN THEY WANT SOMETHING LIGHT. We serve a lot of it at Patsy's. I suggest a nice Linguine with Artichoke Hearts and Olives (page 110) to go with it.

SERVES 4

8 chicken cutlets (about 1½ to 2 pounds), pounded thin, rinsed, and patted dry

½ teaspoon salt, plus more to taste

¼ teaspoon freshly ground black pepper, plus more to taste

½ cup all-purpose flour

¼ cup olive oil

2 tablespoons butter

⅓ cup lemon juice

1¼ cups chicken broth

⅓ cup dry white wine

⅓ cup chopped fresh basil

¾ teaspoon cornstarch

Season the chicken with the salt and pepper and coat with the flour. Heat the oil in a large nonstick skillet over medium flame and sauté the chicken, turning until it is lightly browned on both sides, about 6 minutes.

Drain the oil from the skillet and discard. Add the butter, lemon juice, broth, wine, and basil to the skillet, and bring to a boil. Reduce the heat to medium-low, cover, and simmer for 8 to 10 minutes, or until the chicken is cooked and all ingredients are heated through. Remove the chicken from the skillet and place on a serving platter.

In a small bowl, combine the cornstarch with ¼ cup cold water and mix. Whisk the cornstarch mixture into the pan juices and simmer over low heat until the sauce has thickened, about 1 minute. Season with additional salt and pepper to taste. Place the chicken on a serving platter and spoon the sauce over chicken before serving.

CHICKEN WITH
MUSHROOMS
AND RED PEPPERS

YOU CAN PURCHASE CHICKEN BREASTS THAT ARE BONED, SKINNED, AND split, saving you that chore. I prefer chicken breasts rather than chicken cutlets for this dish because the slightly larger pieces make a better carrier for the sauce.

SERVES 4

8 medium white mushrooms (about ¼ pound), cleaned and thinly sliced

2 skinless and boneless chicken breasts (about 1¼ pounds), split and rinsed

½ teaspoon salt, plus more to taste

¼ teaspoon freshly ground black pepper, plus more to taste

½ cup all-purpose flour

½ cup plus 2 tablespoons olive oil

10 garlic cloves, thinly sliced

2 medium red bell peppers, thinly sliced

½ cup chicken broth

½ cup dry white wine

½ teaspoon dried oregano, crumbled

1 tablespoon chopped fresh basil

Bring a pot of water to a boil. Blanch the mushrooms for 2 minutes, drain, and reserve.

Season the chicken with the salt and pepper and coat with the flour. Heat the ½ cup of oil in a large nonstick skillet over medium flame and sauté the chicken for about 6 minutes, or until lightly browned on both sides. Remove the chicken from the skillet and reserve.

Discard all but 2 tablespoons of the oil from skillet, add the garlic, and sauté about 1 to 2 minutes, or until lightly browned. Add the mushrooms and peppers and sauté 1 to 2 minutes. Add the broth, wine, oregano, and basil, and bring to a boil. Return the chicken to the skillet, cover, reduce the heat to low, and simmer for 10 to 12 minutes, or until all ingredients are hot and the chicken is cooked through.

Remove the chicken from the skillet, place on a serving platter, and keep warm. Bring the pan juices to a boil until the sauce is reduced by half, about 2 to 3 minutes. Season to taste with additional salt and pepper. Spoon the sauce over and around chicken.

CHICKEN PORTOBELLO

THE PORTOBELLOS ADD A HEARTY TOUCH TO A SIMPLY PREPARED DISH, AND the balsamic vinegar gives the sauce a sweet-and-sour taste—called *agrodolce* in Italian.

SERVES 4

4 large portobello mushroom caps (about ½ pound), rinsed and patted dry

⅓ cup plus 1 tablespoon olive oil

1½ pounds chicken cutlets, rinsed

¼ cup all-purpose flour

8 garlic cloves, thinly sliced

½ cup chicken broth

⅓ cup balsamic vinegar

2 tablespoons dry white wine

¼ cup chopped fresh basil

¼ cup chopped fresh flat-leaf parsley

Salt and freshly ground black pepper, to taste

¾ teaspoon cornstarch

Preheat the oven to 450°F.

Brush the mushrooms with 1 tablespoon of the olive oil and place cap side down on a nonstick baking sheet. Bake in the preheated oven for 12 to 14 minutes. Remove, allow to cool, then slice and reserve.

Coat the chicken with the flour. Heat the remaining oil in a large nonstick skillet over medium flame and sauté the chicken until brown on both sides, about 6 minutes. Remove from the pan and reserve. Lower the heat, add the garlic, and sauté for about 1 to 2 minutes, stirring frequently, until garlic slices are lightly browned. Return the chicken to the skillet and add the broth, vinegar, wine, basil, and parsley. Stir to combine, bring sauce to a simmer, and cover. Cook for 5 to 6 minutes, or until all ingredients are heated through. Season to taste with salt and pepper. Remove the chicken from the pan and place on a serving dish. Spoon mushroom slices around the chicken.

Combine the cornstarch with ¼ cup cold water in a small bowl and mix thoroughly. Whisk the cornstarch mixture into the sauce over medium-high heat for 1 to 2 minutes, stirring until the sauce has thickened. Spoon over the chicken before serving.

SCALOPPINE
DI POLLO ZINGARA

ZINGARA MEANS "GYPSY" IN ITALIAN, AND I HAVE NO IDEA HOW THIS DISH got that name. I'm not sure that cultivated asparagus would have been available to gypsies traveling about in caravans in the countryside, but I'm sure the name has some romantic background to it.

SERVES 4

6 large white mushrooms, cleaned and thinly sliced

6 thin stalks asparagus, washed, trimmed, and sliced on the diagonal into 1-inch pieces

8 chicken cutlets (about 1½ pounds), pounded thin and rinsed

½ cup all-purpose flour

¼ cup olive oil

1 small yellow onion, thinly sliced

1 large red bell pepper, thinly sliced

6 artichoke hearts, canned in water, drained and quartered

3 scallions (white and green parts), thinly sliced

¼ cup chopped fresh basil

¼ cup chopped fresh flat-leaf parsley

½ teaspoon dried rosemary, crushed

1½ cups chicken broth

¼ cup dry white wine

1 tablespoon butter

Salt and freshly ground black pepper, to taste

Bring a large pot of water to a boil, add the mushrooms and the asparagus, and blanch for 2 minutes. Drain and reserve.

Coat the chicken with flour. Heat the oil in a large nonstick skillet over medium-high flame and sauté the chicken until lightly browned on both sides, turning once, about 6 minutes. Remove from the skillet and reserve.

Add more oil to the skillet if necessary and sauté the onion over medium-high heat until lightly browned, about 5 minutes. Add the red bell pepper, artichoke hearts, and reserved mushrooms and asparagus. Stir to combine, reduce heat to medium, and sauté for 3 minutes. Return the chicken and add the scallions, basil, parsley, rosemary, broth, wine, and butter. Season with salt and pepper. Reduce the heat, cover, and simmer until the chicken is cooked through and all of the ingredients are hot, about 8 to 10 minutes.

Kaye Ballard

"I first encountered Patsy's Restaurant about forty years ago. I went there with Larry Storch. We had a wonderful waiter wearing a gray busboy's jacket. He was so attentive and generous, bringing samples of different dishes he felt we had to try. It wasn't until a few years later that we found out he was the owner—Patsy Scognamillo—and I've been going back to Patsy's ever since.

"Being Italian, Patsy's is my home cook-ing away from home cooking—the best Italian food I've found in New York City. And it's a gathering place for so many show-biz people who love good Italian food.

"Thank you, Joe, and your son, Sal (the master chef). And I thank Patsy's daughter, Anna, and her son, Frank, for carrying on the wonderful tradition that dear Patsy started. Love and God bless you all."

ROLLATINI DI PETTO
DI POLLO E SPINACI

PREPARING THIS DISH WITH FROZEN SPINACH AT HOME SAVES TIME AND ALL the bother of rinsing and draining fresh spinach. These chicken rolls are festive and appealing, and wonderful with a pasta tossed with vodka sauce.

SERVES 4

6 large white mushrooms

¼ cup plus 2 tablespoons olive oil

4 garlic cloves, minced

1 10-ounce package chopped frozen spinach, cooked according to package directions and drained

⅔ cup freshly grated Parmigiano-Reggiano

Salt and freshly ground black pepper, to taste

2 boneless and skinless chicken breasts (about 1¼ pounds), split and pounded thin

2 medium eggs, lightly beaten

½ cup Seasoned Bread Crumbs (page 49)

Bring a large pot of water to a boil, add the mushrooms, and blanch for 2 minutes. Drain, chop fine, and reserve.

Heat ¼ cup of the oil in a large nonstick skillet over medium flame and sauté the garlic until just golden, about 1 to 2 minutes. Add the chopped mushrooms and cooked spinach and continue cooking for 2 to 3 minutes, or until any liquid has evaporated. Transfer the spinach-mushroom mixture to a bowl and refrigerate for 1 hour, or until cool. Stir in the cheese, season to taste with salt and pepper, and mix thoroughly.

Preheat the oven to 500°F.

Place a quarter of the stuffing on the lower third of each cutlet and roll, tucking in the ends and sides. Season with salt and pepper. Coat the chicken rolls with the beaten egg, and then with the bread crumbs, covering completely. Coat a baking pan with the remaining 2 tablespoons oil and arrange the rolls in one layer. Bake for 20 to 24 minutes, turning once or twice, until rolls are browned on all sides. Serve immediately.

HERB-ROASTED CHICKEN

TO ENSURE A ROASTED CHICKEN THAT'S CRISP ON THE OUTSIDE BUT NOT dry within, you should turn the bird every ten minutes or so, allowing it to become coated with the oil and the other liquids in the roasting pan. It wouldn't hurt to do a little basting as well.

SERVES 4

1 3- to 3½- pound chicken, quartered

¼ cup olive oil, plus 2 tablespoons for
    greasing pan

1 teaspoon salt, plus more to taste

½ teaspoon freshly ground black pepper,
    plus more to taste

4 scallions (white and green parts),
    chopped

1 sprig fresh rosemary, chopped

8 large basil leaves, chopped

2 tablespoons unsalted butter

¾ cup chicken broth

¼ cup Madeira wine

Preheat the oven to 500°F.

Coat a roasting pan with 2 tablespoons of the oil. Place the chicken in the roasting pan, season with the salt and pepper, drizzle with the remaining oil, and roast for 30 minutes, turning every 10 minutes to brown on all sides. Add the scallions, rosemary, basil, butter, broth, and Madeira to the pan, and roast for an additional 15 or 20 minutes, or until chicken is cooked through. Remove the chicken from roasting pan and keep warm.

Scrape up the browned bits from the bottom of the pan and transfer with the juices to a saucepan. Bring the liquid to a boil and cook over high heat until sauce is reduced and has thickened slightly. Season with salt and pepper to taste. Place the chicken on a serving platter and spoon with sauce before serving.

CHICKEN LIVERS
WITH PEPPERS

LOOK TO YOUR BUTCHER WHEN PURCHASING CHICKEN LIVERS. THEY SHOULD be fresh, fresh, *fresh*. Chicken livers are delicate and spoil quickly, so you want to make sure that the livers have not been sitting around in a meat case for days or even weeks.

Wash the livers thoroughly and pat dry. Remove any bits of fat, and if the veins connecting the two lobes of each liver seem especially large, cut the liver in two and discard the connecting tissue.

SERVES 4

1½ pounds chicken livers

½ cup olive oil

8 garlic cloves, thinly sliced

2 cups canned Italian plum tomatoes, with juice

1 large red bell pepper, thinly sliced

½ cup chicken broth

Pinch of oregano

2 tablespoons chopped fresh flat-leaf parsley

Salt and freshly ground black pepper, to taste

Wash the chicken livers and pat dry.

Heat ¼ cup of the oil in a large nonstick skillet over medium-high flame and sauté the livers for about 10 minutes, or until brown on all sides and cooked through. Using a slotted spatula, remove the livers from the skillet and drain on paper towels. Reserve.

Discard the used oil from the skillet, add the remaining oil, and heat over medium flame. Sauté the garlic for 1 to 2 minutes, or until lightly golden. Add the tomatoes, cover, reduce the heat to medium, and simmer for 15 minutes.

Add the pepper slices, chicken broth, and the oregano, and cook an additional 10 minutes. Return the livers to skillet and add the parsley. Cook until livers are heated through, about 4 to 5 minutes. Season with salt and pepper.

THE *Garlic* STORY

Italian cooking is rich with garlic. The most important thing to remember is not to let garlic burn. This can pose a problem for those people who may be allergic to garlic, and others who know—or perhaps just think—that they don't like it. If you like garlic but believe it causes indigestion, here's how I handled that problem for Frank Sinatra and now for my father, Joe: I leave small cloves whole, or cut large cloves in half, and sauté the garlic in the oil I will be using for the dish. When the garlic is a light brown, I remove it from the oil and toss it away. Then I continue with the dish using the garlic-flavored oil, but without the garlic itself.

Nathan "Sonny" Golden

"Frank Sinatra first brought me to Patsy's, and I still remember that I was greeted at the door by himself—Patsy Scognamillo," shares Sonny Golden, Frank Sinatra's friend and accountant. "I love the whole family, and I go there as often as I can because the food is great, and Sal and Joe, Frank and Anna—they all make me feel like part of the family."

CHICKEN VENEZIANA

HERE'S ANOTHER FINE EXAMPLE OF THE ITALIAN SWEET-AND-SOUR TECHNIQUE —*agrodolce*—in which balsamic vinegar is used to impart a special flavor to a dish.

SERVES 4

½ pound white mushrooms, cleaned and thinly sliced

8 chicken cutlets (about 1½ to 2 pounds), pounded thin and rinsed

½ teaspoon salt, plus more to taste

¼ teaspoon freshly ground black pepper, plus more to taste

½ cup all-purpose flour

¼ cup olive oil

2 medium yellow onions, thinly sliced

1 cup chicken broth

¼ cup balsamic vinegar

2 tablespoons butter

1 tablespoon chopped fresh flat-leaf parsley

⅓ cup chopped fresh basil

¾ teaspoon cornstarch

Bring a pot of water to a boil. Blanch the mushrooms for 2 minutes, drain, and reserve.

Season the chicken with salt and pepper and coat with flour. Heat the oil in a large nonstick skillet over medium-high flame and sauté the chicken until lightly browned on both sides, turning once, about 6 minutes. Remove from the skillet and reserve. Add the onions and sauté until they just start to brown, about 4 to 5 minutes. Return the chicken and add the blanched mushrooms, broth, vinegar, and butter, increase the flame to high, and bring to a boil. Reduce the heat to low, cover, and simmer for 8 minutes, stirring occasionally, until chicken is cooked through. Add the parsley and basil, stir to combine, and simmer for 1 additional minute. Remove the chicken from the skillet and place on a serving platter.

Combine the cornstarch with ¼ cup cold water. Mix well, whisk into the pan juices, and simmer until the sauce has thickened slightly, 1 to 2 minutes. Season to taste with salt and pepper. Place the chicken on a serving platter and pour sauce over.

Phil Rizzuto
BASEBALL'S FAMOUS "SCOOTER"

"I've been going to Patsy's Restaurant since the 1950s when I was with the Yankees. Holy cow, it's such a great place: the warm atmosphere, the ambiance, and let's talk about the food! I'm crazy about the Pasta Fazool —even though they write it 'Pasta e Fagioli' on the menu. And I love the fish and the Linguine with Red Clam Sauce. I'm not in New York all the time, but whenever I come to town Patsy's is one of my first and favorite stops. You'll find me there with my wife, and my good friend and manager, Michael Amato. Patsy's is like the Yankees—a real winner."

"Thanks, Sal, for the many entertaining evenings I have spent at Patsy's Restaurant. I look forward to many more in the future."

—BRIAN M. CASHMAN, YANKEES GENERAL MANAGER

6

"OUR MEAT DISHES ARE NOT FOR TIMID EATERS," SAYS JOE. "Portions are large and flavors intense. We have cut down on the amounts for the meat dishes in this book. But if you're having Al Pacino to dinner, you better make sure you have a three-inch-thick veal chop. When I see him come into the restaurant, I head for the kitchen to tell Sal to get ready to prepare one of those chops. It's his favorite."

It's a favorite for many of our guests, and it's made with the best quality veal, roasted, with a reduction of oil, garlic, rosemary, and balsamic vinegar added during the last few minutes of cooking— that's Sicilian style.

The main way to ensure that meat dishes are special is to simply buy the best meat. Our veal is the best that money can buy, and the beef is prime. We purchase baby lamb and free-range chicken. Get to know your butcher—you're halfway home when you start with the best ingredients.

MEATS

FILET MIGNON BAROLO

MANZO ALLA SICILIANO

STEAK ALLA PATSY

ROASTED RACK OF LAMB

HOT SAUSAGES SAN GENNARO

PORK TENDERLOIN WITH PORT

PORK CHOPS WITH VINEGAR PEPPERS

SPEZZATINO DI VITELLO

BRACIOLETTINI DI VITELLO

VEAL MARSALA

FILET MIGNON BAROLO

BAROLO IS ONE OF THE FINEST RED WINES PRODUCED IN ITALY. IT COMES from the Piedmont region and is robust and full-bodied. If you wish, you may substitute a Chianti Classico for the Barolo in this recipe.

SERVES 4

½ pound white mushrooms, cleaned and
   thinly sliced
¼ cup olive oil, plus more for coating pan
1 medium yellow onion, chopped
⅛ pound prosciutto, finely chopped
⅓ cup beef broth

½ cup Barolo wine
2 tablespoons unsalted butter
¼ cup chopped fresh flat-leaf parsley
Salt and freshly ground black pepper,
   to taste
4 slices filet mignon, each about 8 ounces

Preheat the oven to 500°F.

Bring a medium pot of water to a boil. Add the mushrooms and blanch for 2 minutes. Drain and reserve.

Heat the oil in a large nonstick skillet over medium flame and sauté the onion, stirring occasionally, until lightly browned, about 3 minutes. Add the prosciutto and the blanched mushroom slices, and sauté for 2 minutes. Add the beef broth, wine, butter, and parsley, and stir to combine. Bring to a boil, reduce heat to low, and allow the sauce to simmer for 3 to 4 minutes. Season to taste with salt and pepper. Remove from the heat and reserve.

Lightly oil a roasting pan large enough to hold the meat in one layer. Sprinkle the filets with salt and pepper, place in the pan, and roast in the preheated oven, turning once, for 15 to 16 minutes for medium rare (about 150°F. internal temperature). Drain the oil from the pan and discard. Spoon the sauce over the filets, and roast for an additional 2 to 3 minutes, or until sauce is hot. Serve immediately.

Cindy Adams

"I've been going to Patsy's Restaurant longer than I admit I'm old. My husband took me there originally with Frank Sinatra. Go there now and you see such celebrities as Tony Bennett, Rush Limbaugh, Joan Lunden, Jennifer Lopez, and Puff Daddy.

"Pasquale [Patsy] originally befriended Frank in the hungry days, something that Frank never forgot. And Patsy's will forever be home to every Sinatra—and Sinatra fan—including me.

"Why do we hang out there? Because it was Sinatra's place, sure. But also because the food is great and the Scognamillo family makes you feel like you're family—theirs. If I'm feeling down (yes, it does happen) I know Patsy's will cheer me. If I'm feeling up, Patsy's will help me celebrate. It's part of me, part of my New York."

Joe remembers: "It was a sad day—the day of Joey Adams' funeral—and I'll never forget that when Cindy spoke, she acknowledged my presence and the fact that I took care of her husband whenever he came to Patsy's and mentioned the many years that she and I had been close friends. There were many dignitaries present, including Senator Hillary Clinton, and I was honored at being singled out."

MANZO ALLA SICILIANO

MANZO MEANS BEEF IN ITALIAN, AND THIS DISH, SERVED WITH A RED sauce, is quite popular in southern Italy. We prepare it at our restaurant with an expensive cut of meat, but it can also be made with chuck steaks, pounded thin, or skirt steak, broiled and then thinly sliced.

SERVES 4

1 large carrot, diced

8 large white mushrooms, cleaned and
    thinly sliced

3 tablespoons olive oil, plus more for
    coating roasting pan

1 leek (white part only), washed and
    thinly sliced

2 scallions (white and green parts), thinly
    sliced

2 cloves garlic, minced

1 16-ounce can whole plum tomatoes,
    with juice

1/2 cup beef broth

Pinch of sage

1 teaspoon salt

1/2 teaspoon freshly ground black pepper

4 medallions of beef, or 4 beef filets,
    about 8 ounces each, 1 3/4 inches thick

Preheat the oven to 500°F.

Bring a medium pot of water to a boil. Add the carrots and the mushrooms, and blanch for 2 minutes. Drain and reserve.

Heat the oil in a large saucepan over medium flame and sauté the leek and scallions until just soft, about 3 minutes. Add the garlic and sauté for 1 minute, until golden. Coarsely chop the tomatoes and add with their juice to the saucepan. Bring to a boil, reduce the heat to low, cover, and simmer for 15 minutes. Add the beef broth, reserved carrots and mushrooms, and sage. Bring to a boil, cover, reduce heat to low, and simmer for 10 minutes. Season with 1/2 teaspoon salt and 1/4 teaspoon pepper. Keep warm over very low heat.

Lightly oil a roasting pan large enough to hold the meat in one layer. Season the filets with the remaining ½ teaspoon salt and ¼ teaspoon pepper, place in the pan, and roast in the oven, turning once, for 15 to 16 minutes for medium rare (the meat should reach an internal temperature of 150°F.). Drain the oil from the pan and discard. Spoon a small amount of the sauce on a serving platter, place the beef on top, and spoon the remaining sauce over meat.

THE *Endless Kitchen*

"I learned when I was growing up," says Joey, "that a kitchen is endless—there is no bottom to it. By that I mean every morsel of food can be used, extended, eaten with joy. We didn't have too many meat dishes as such—no big steaks or chops—but my mother could do wonderful things with a small amount of meat. She would take inexpensive cuts of meat—short ribs, a tough piece of chuck—and she would cook it into a delicious soup. The next day the meat would appear in another form: It would be braised, a sauce added, and served with pasta.

"And then my mother used cuts of meat that are not favored today: A beef heart, for example, could be cooked until tender, sliced, and cooked again in a sauce, and it was enough to serve our whole family. We loved tripe, not just the honeycomb that is eaten today, but all types of tripe. My mother also made something she called a *soffritto*—I know the same word is used in Latino cooking, where it means a spicy sauce used to flavor food. But for us, a soffritto was a combination of such innards as the liver and heart, which were boiled together until tender, cubed, and then sautéed with a little onion, salt and pepper, and tomato paste. Delicious! As was the Neapolitan dish that combined tripe, brains, and peas. For some reason, that dish was very popular with singers who came from Italy. I remember my father telling me that it was a favorite of Enrico Caruso."

Roger Ailes

"I've been a Patsy's devotee since 1964, and one of my proudest boasts is that I brought Rush Limbaugh to the restaurant the very first time he ate there," claims Ailes, the head of Fox News. "Of course, the rest is history as far as Rush is concerned—he loves the place and the whole Scognamillo family. But what's hard about that? Everyone who knows them loves them. They're the family that used to be a staple on television: loving, caring, interested in your welfare. Not too many people like that around anymore, not on television or in real life. But they can be found at Patsy's Restaurant. And in addition to all the TLC they give you, they can cook—and how! My favorite dish—though I've got to say I never had a dish at Patsy's that I didn't like—is their Steak alla Patsy."

"You always meet interesting people at Patsy's . . . I once met a Godfather there. But the real reason I go there is because of the ambiance, the feeling of family."

—FLORENCE HENDERSON

STEAK
ALLA PATSY

WHY DOES EVERYONE LOVE OUR STEAKS? AFTER ALL, WE'RE A SOUTHERN Italian, red-sauce restaurant, not a steak house. First of all, we use prime beef. And then we serve it with our very special sauce. This is steak plus! Prepare it at home and you'll also get raves. The steaks can also be pan-broiled on top of the stove, instead of in the broiler.

SERVES 2 TO 4

4 slices bacon, diced small

¼ cup olive oil

1 medium yellow onion, thinly sliced

4 scallions (white and green parts), thinly
    sliced

2 tablespoons fresh chopped basil

½ cup chicken broth

¼ cup dry white wine

½ teaspoon salt

¼ teaspoon freshly ground black pepper

2 sirloin steaks, each 1¼ pounds,
    1¼ inches thick

Preheat the broiler.

Heat a large nonstick skillet over low flame. Add the bacon and sauté until crisp, about 4 to 5 minutes. Remove the bacon with a slotted spoon and set on paper towels to drain. Remove and discard the bacon fat, wipe the pan clean, add the oil, and return to the low flame. Add the onion and sauté until soft and almost caramelized, about 10 minutes. Add the reserved bacon, scallions, basil, broth, and wine. Add ½ teaspoon salt and ¼ teaspoon pepper. Bring to a boil, reduce the heat to low, and simmer until the liquid is reduced by half, about 2 to 3 minutes. Remove from heat.

Place the steaks in the preheated broiler about 3 inches from heat, and broil, turning once, to the desired degree of doneness. Place the broiled steaks on a platter, and pour sauce over steaks.

ROASTED
RACK OF LAMB

IN ITALY, LAMB IS A SEASONAL DISH. IT'S USUALLY SERVED IN THE SPRING and is a special treat at Easter. Here in the United States, fine lamb is available year-round. This is our version of Agnello Arrosto, Italian roast lamb. We prepare it with racks of baby lamb—which is the most delicate lamb available—and we trim the fat and meat off the end of each rib bone, leaving a dramatically exposed length of bone at each chop. Your butcher will do this for you—it's a procedure called frenching the chops. (We'd rather it was called italianing the chops, but that's the way it is.)

SERVES 4

2 racks of baby lamb (about 1 pound
    each), trimmed and frenched

½ teaspoon salt, plus more to taste

¼ teaspoon freshly ground black pepper,
    plus more to taste

¼ cup olive oil

3 scallions (white and green parts),
    chopped

1 sprig fresh rosemary, chopped

4 leaves fresh basil, chopped

2 tablespoons unsalted butter

½ cup chicken broth

¼ cup dry white wine

½ teaspoon cornstarch

Preheat the oven to 500°F.

Season the lamb with the ½ teaspoon salt and ¼ teaspoon pepper. Lightly oil a roasting pan with 1 tablespoon of the olive oil. Place the lamb in the pan and spoon the remaining oil over the lamb. Roast for 20 minutes, turning once. Drain and discard the oil from the pan.

Add the scallions, rosemary, basil, butter, broth, and wine to the pan. Return to the oven and roast an additional 10 minutes for medium lamb (it should reach about 165°F. internal temperature). Remove the lamb from the oven and place on a serving platter.

Scrape up the brown bits from the bottom of the roaster and transfer with pan juices to a small saucepan. Bring to a boil over high heat and cook for 2 to 5 minutes, or until the sauce has reduced by one third.

In a small bowl, combine the cornstarch with ¼ cup water. Mix well and whisk into the sauce. Bring to a simmer and cook for about 3 minutes, or until the sauce has thickened slightly. Season to taste with salt and pepper.

Carve the lamb into individual chops and pour sauce over chops.

HOT SAUSAGES
SAN GENNARO

IF YOU'RE SERVING PEOPLE WITH BIG APPETITES, THIS DISH MAKES A GREAT
starter. But it's also good as a main dish; I like to have it after a salad followed by fruit
for dessert—maybe poached pears with a few maddalena cookies.

SERVES 4 TO 6

12 links (about 2½ pounds) fresh, hot
   Italian sausages

6 tablespoons olive oil

2 medium yellow onions, thinly sliced

1 14-ounce can Italian whole plum
   tomatoes, with juice

6 hot vinegar cherry peppers, seeded and
   thinly sliced

1 teaspoon crushed red pepper flakes

Salt and freshly ground black pepper,
   to taste

1 tablespoon tomato paste (optional)

2 tablespoons chopped fresh basil

2 tablespoons chopped fresh flat-leaf
   parsley

Puncture the sausages in several places with a fork. Heat two tablespoons of the oil in
a large nonstick skillet over low flame, add the sausages, and sauté, turning frequently
to brown on all sides, until cooked through, about 15 to 18 minutes. Remove from the
skillet and drain on paper towels. Discard the oil from the skillet.

Heat the remaining 4 tablespoons of oil in the skillet over medium flame and sauté
the onions for 3 to 4 minutes, or until the onions are translucent and lightly golden.
Coarsely chop the tomatoes and add with their juice and bring to a boil. Reduce the
heat to low, cover, and simmer for 25 minutes, stirring occasionally. Return the sausages
to the sauce, add the cherry peppers and red pepper flakes, cover, and continue to simmer for 15 minutes, or until flavors have blended.

Season to taste with salt and pepper. Stir in the tomato paste (if using) and add the
basil and parsley. Simmer uncovered for 2 minutes. Serve hot.

ROSE MEETS *Frank Sinatra*

"I haven't worked at Patsy's for as long as my husband, Joe, or the others in the family. I was home raising Sal and his sister, and for years I kept hearing about Frank Sinatra without ever meeting him. And then one day, after I had started working at the restaurant, I learned that Frank Sinatra would be having dinner at Patsy's.

"'Joey,' I said, 'I want to meet Frank Sinatra!'

"The restaurant was really busy that day, and when Joey finally remembered, Frank was getting ready to leave.

"'Come on, Rose,' Joey said, 'we'll wait for him by the side staircase, and I'll introduce you.'

"I went outside with Joe, and as usual when people knew that Frank Sinatra was around, a crowd formed. A group of women were waiting by the front door. Now, I'm not really a pushy person, but this one time I did manage to elbow myself forward. When Frank came down the stairs and opened that side door, I was standing right there.

"'Frank,' Joey said, 'I'd like you to meet my wife—this is Rose.'

"Frank smiled, took a step forward, hugged me, and gave me a kiss. We looked at each other, and I could see why people made such a fuss about his eyes—they were a wonderful, penetrating blue. 'Joey,' Frank said, 'you're a lucky guy, she's beautiful.' There was one more hug, and his security people surrounded him and got him to his limo. I had waited for years to meet Frank Sinatra, and it was worth the wait."

PORK
TENDERLOIN WITH PORT

TENDERLOIN, A BONELESS CUT OF PORK, IS QUICK AND EASY TO PREPARE.
Its long and narrow shape cooks quickly and there's less chance of the meat drying out
and becoming tough. Here, the pork is served with a simple wine sauce—we prefer ruby
port, but you could substitute a tawny, which has a lighter, fresher taste.

SERVES 4

1½ to 2 pounds pork tenderloin, about
   2½ inches thick

2 tablespoons olive oil

½ teaspoon salt, plus more to taste

¼ teaspoon freshly ground black pepper,
   plus more to taste

4 scallions (white and green parts),
   chopped

1 tablespoon chopped fresh basil

1 tablespoon chopped fresh flat-leaf
   parsley

2 sprigs fresh rosemary, chopped

⅓ cup chicken broth

½ cup ruby port

2 bay leaves

2 tablespoons unsalted butter

1 teaspoon cornstarch

Preheat the oven to 500°F. Coat the pork with oil, and season with the salt and pepper.
Place the pork in a roasting pan and roast in the preheated oven for 10 minutes. Turn
and roast for an additional 8 minutes, or until brown. Drain and discard the oil.

Add the scallions, basil, parsley, rosemary, broth, port, bay leaves, and butter to the
pan, and roast an additional 4 minutes, or until cooked through (to an internal temperature of 175°F.). Remove the pork and place on a serving platter.

Pour the pan juices into a medium saucepan and bring to a simmer over medium
heat. Remove and discard the bay leaves. Combine the cornstarch and ¼ cup cold water
in a bowl, mix until thoroughly combined, and whisk into sauce. Cook for 2 minutes,
or until sauce has thickened slightly. Season to taste. Slice the pork and spoon sauce
over the meat.

Jackie Gleason
AND THE ROAST SUCKLING PIG

"We cook for a lot of celebrities," says Joe Scognamillo. "I mean, people who want us to prepare meals and then deliver it—or they send someone to pick it up. A lot of stars are busy doing television or movies, recordings, they have rehearsals, they're too tired to come to the restaurant, but they still want our food. I took food regularly to Frank Sinatra when he was singing at the Paramount. When Jennifer Lopez was doing *Saturday Night Live* she sent over for some of her favorite dishes. We deliver to Tony Bennett when he's here doing a recording session.

"We used to deliver dinners nightly to Jackie Gleason when he was doing his television show. I would do anything for Jackie Gleason. Too many people identify an actor with the part he plays, but Jackie was one of the politest, most elegant men I've ever met. He dressed well, too, usually wore a diamond stickpin in his tie. Anyway, he was staying at a hotel nearby and I'd prepare whatever he wanted—a prime rib, Veal Pizzaiola, whatever.

"And then one day he asked, 'Could you make me a suckling pig?' 'Sure,' I told him, 'why not, just give me some advance notice because I have to order it.' He called a few days later, and I ordered the meat and called Jackie to tell him I had it. 'Fine,' he said, 'and with it I want you to send a big bowl of mashed potatoes. A big bowl of sauerkraut, a big bowl of baked beans.' I guess he must have named five different things.

"I roasted the pig, fixed it up real nice, you know—apple in its mouth and everything. And I prepared all the other things he had ordered. Jackie Gleason had a duplex apartment at a hotel nearby, and when I called him he said, 'You know the way. Just bring everything over and put it in the kitchen.'

"I got a couple of guys from the restaurant to help me and we carried up everything to his apartment and laid it out, all nice, in the kitchen. When Jackie Gleason walked in I asked, 'When is your company coming, Mr. Gleason?'

"And Jackie Gleason said, 'What company?' I couldn't believe it, but when I went back to pick up the bowls they were all empty, and the only thing on the platter was a pile of bones.

"Every time I look at Jackie's picture on our Wall of Fame, I'm moved by what he wrote: 'Patsy's was the best, is the best, always will be the best.'"

PORK CHOPS
WITH VINEGAR PEPPERS

BECAUSE OF THE DEMANDS OF THE AMERICAN PUBLIC FOR LESS FAT AND leaner meat, ranchers have developed pork that is lean—too lean, according to many people who understand fine food. Lean pork can also mean tough pork. To avoid this, be sure not to overcook. Cook until pork is tender when pierced with a fork and juices run clear.

SERVES 4

¼ cup olive oil, plus more for coating pan

4 center-cut rib pork chops, each
    1½ inches thick (about 2 pounds)

8 garlic cloves, thinly sliced

8 vinegar cherry peppers (about
    1½ cups), seeded and thinly sliced

¼ cup chicken broth

¼ cup dry white wine

4 tablespoons balsamic vinegar

8 large basil leaves

2 tablespoons finely chopped fresh
    flat-leaf parsley

Salt and freshly ground black pepper,
    to taste

Preheat the oven to 475°F.

Lightly oil a nonstick roasting pan with 2 tablespoons of the olive oil. Place the chops in the pan and roast in the preheated oven for 8 to 9 minutes. Turn and roast for 7 to 8 minutes on the second side.

Meanwhile, heat the ¼ cup olive oil in a medium saucepan over low flame. Add garlic and sauté for about 2 minutes, or until lightly browned. Add the peppers, broth, wine, vinegar, basil, and parsley to the saucepan. Bring to a simmer and cook for 2 minutes. Season to taste with salt and pepper.

Drain and discard the oil from the roasting pan. Pour the sauce over and around the chops and continue roasting for 6 minutes, or until chops are cooked through (they should reach an internal temperature of 185°F.). Transfer the chops to a serving platter or individual dinner plates and spoon sauce over chops.

SPEZZATINO DI VITELLO

THIS FLAVORFUL VEAL STEW CAN BE PREPARED A DAY IN ADVANCE, AND then reheated before serving. I think veal shoulder is the best cut for this dish, but shanks may be substituted.

SERVES 4

2½ pounds veal shoulder, boned, cut into
    2-inch cubes

1 teaspoon salt, plus more to taste

½ teaspoon freshly ground black pepper,
    plus more to taste

½ cup all-purpose flour

⅔ cup olive oil

2 medium yellow onions, chopped

6 celery ribs, chopped

2 cups canned Italian plum tomatoes,
    coarsely chopped, with juice

½ cup plus 2 tablespoons dry white wine

¼ cup chopped fresh flat-leaf parsley

4 bay leaves

3 carrots, halved lengthwise then cut into
    1-inch pieces

3 medium potatoes, peeled and cut into
    1-inch cubes

Season the cubed veal with the salt and pepper, and coat with flour.

Heat the oil in a Dutch oven over medium flame and sauté the veal, turning, until brown on all sides, about 6 minutes. Remove the veal and reserve.

Add more oil to the Dutch oven if it's dry, and heat for 1 minute. Reduce the flame to low and sauté the onions and celery, stirring occasionally, for about 5 minutes, or until the vegetables are golden. Return the veal and add the tomatoes, ½ cup of the wine, the parsley, bay leaves, and enough water to cover (at least 2 cups). Bring to a boil, reduce the heat to low, and cover. Simmer for 1 hour and 30 minutes, stirring occasionally and adding water as necessary.

Add the carrots and potatoes and cook for 20 to 25 minutes, until the veal and vegetables are fork tender. Add the remaining wine, bring to a boil, and remove from the heat. Discard the bay leaves, season to taste with salt and pepper, and serve.

BRACIOLETTINI DI VITELLO

BRACIOLE—ROLLS MADE OF BEEF AND STUFFED—IS THE LARGER, HEAVIER relative of these smaller and more delicate rolls or packages made with veal. These Braciolettini demand quick cooking, and I think they're best served after a hearty soup.

SERVES 4

8 thin slices veal scaloppine, about
  1¼ pounds

¼ teaspoon salt

¼ teaspoon black pepper

1 cup shredded mozzarella cheese
  (about ½ pound)

⅔ cup freshly grated Parmigiano-
  Reggiano

8 large basil leaves

8 strips bacon

1 tablespoon olive oil

Preheat the oven to 475°F.

Sprinkle the veal with the salt and pepper. In a medium bowl, combine the mozzarella and the Parmigiano-Reggiano, and mix. Form the cheese combination into 8 balls, each about 1 inch in diameter.

Lay the veal slices on a work surface. Place a basil leaf and a cheese ball on the bottom third of each veal slice. Roll the veal slices, tucking in sides and ends as you roll, to make a tight packet. Wrap a bacon strip diagonally around each veal roll. Secure with a toothpick.

Coat an ovenproof baking dish lightly with the olive oil and arrange the veal rolls in one layer on baking dish. Bake for 10 minutes. Turn the rolls and bake an additional 9 minutes, or until the veal is lightly browned and the bacon is crisp. Remove the toothpicks and serve.

Debbie Allen

"I first came to Patsy's Restaurant at the invitation of Sammy Davis Jr. We were shooting an Alka-Seltzer commercial. After shooting just one take, he took the entire cast to Patsy's for lunch. I had the Chopped Salad and the Veal Piccata and tasted every dessert off the tray. That was back in 1977, and Patsy's has remained my favorite New York restaurant since that time. The food is divine, the cocktails superior, especially the Cosmopolitans."

"*Patsy's* is the old New York, the best New York, and a throwback to my mother's Italian feasts from yesterday."

—REGIS PHILBIN

VEAL MARSALA

AN ELEGANT YET SIMPLE DISH, VEAL MARSALA CAN BE PREPARED QUICKLY and is fine for company when you don't want to spend too much time in the kitchen. If you wish, you can prepare this dish in advance.

SERVES 4

12 medium white mushrooms, cleaned
    and thinly sliced

¼ cup olive oil

8 thin slices veal scaloppine (about
    1¼ pounds)

4 scallions (white and green parts), finely
    chopped

⅓ cup sweet Marsala wine

½ cup beef broth

1 tablespoon chopped fresh basil

1 tablespoon unsalted butter

Salt and freshly ground black pepper,
    to taste

Bring a medium pot of water to a boil, add the mushrooms, blanch for 2 minutes, drain, and reserve.

Heat the olive oil in a large skillet over medium-high flame and sauté the veal until browned on both sides, about 6 minutes total. Remove the veal, cover lightly with aluminum foil, and keep warm. Reduce the heat to medium and sauté the scallions for 2 to 3 minutes, or until soft. Add the blanched mushrooms and continue to cook and stir for 3 minutes, or until mushrooms have browned. Return the veal to the skillet and add the wine, ⅓ cup of the beef broth, basil, butter, and salt and pepper to taste. Bring to a boil, reduce the heat to low, cover, and simmer for 6 to 8 minutes, adding more broth if necessary.

Our Photographs

"Most show-business people love having their pictures on our Wall of Fame," says Anna. "We got Sylvester Stallone's picture from his mother. He's a regular here, but he always forgot to bring in his photo. His mother was here one night and wanted to know how come her son's picture wasn't on our wall. I explained that he hadn't sent us one, so she said, 'Never mind.' And then the picture arrived signed by Sylvester Stallone.

"Our wall has so many of our guests pictured there: Gregory Peck, Roger Moore, Dom DeLuise, Neil Sedaka, Fred Astaire—unfortunately, he couldn't sign his name because his hands were swollen with arthritis. We have just about everyone.

"Jackie Gleason overheard some people one night who were looking at his picture—an old one—and he heard them say, 'He sure doesn't look like that anymore.' He sent us a more recent picture.

"And then there was the time Burt Lancaster was sitting at the bar, and some people looked at his picture on the wall and said, 'That's probably one of those pictures you can buy—Burt Lancaster has probably never eaten here.' Burt turned on his barstool and smiled. He made sure that those people saw him. They were so flustered they didn't know what to say."

7

THIS CHAPTER INCLUDES MANY OF THE OLD FAVORITES such as an easy Lobster Fra Diavolo, and there are shrimp dishes that can be served as starters as well as main courses. We've also made some recent additions to our seafood selection. For example, many of my customers asked for Chilean sea bass, so I developed a recipe and added eggplant and olives to give it an Italian flavor.

Fish is increasingly popular—many people see it as less fattening than other protein dishes. I recommend you add one or two fishes to your repertoire. They're usually not difficult to prepare; the secret is to buy fish that is really fresh. Get to know your fishmonger. Find food shops that you can rely on, and let them get to know you, your likes, dislikes, and requirements. Start out with the best ingredients, and they will be reflected in the dinner you put on the table.

FISH AND SHELLFISH

SAL'S CHILEAN SEA BASS WITH EGGPLANT
AND OLIVES

CASSUOLA DI CALAMARI

FILLET OF SOLE ARREGANATA

TROTA ALLA GIARDINO

ROASTED STRIPED BASS WITH
HORSERADISH CRUST

PROSCIUTTO-WRAPPED MONKFISH

SALMON WITH HERB SAUCE

SAUTÉED SHRIMP WITH COGNAC AND
DIJON MUSTARD

CALAMARI SALAD

SHRIMP MILANESE

SHRIMP SCAMPI

SWORDFISH STEAKS ARREGANATA

MARINATED TUNA STEAKS WITH
CILANTRO SAUCE

SAL'S
CHILEAN SEA BASS
WITH EGGPLANT AND OLIVES

THIS IS NOT AN OLD NEAPOLITAN RECIPE HANDED DOWN BY MY GRAND-father, but something I created because so many of my customers were asking for Chilean sea bass, which is really Patagonian toothfish. If you don't care for Chilean sea bass, no matter what it's called, you can serve this sauce with cod, scrod, or sole. Just be sure to have the sauce prepared before you cook the fish.

SERVES 4

SAUCE

2 small Italian eggplants, about ½ pound, peeled and cut into ½-inch cubes

½ cup olive oil

8 garlic cloves, chopped

1 medium red bell pepper, thinly sliced

2 tablespoons chopped fresh basil

2 anchovy fillets in oil, drained and finely chopped

2 tablespoons capers, rinsed and drained

16 kalamata or gaeta olives, pitted and sliced

2 tablespoons chopped fresh flat-leaf parsley

1 14-ounce can plum tomatoes, with juice

Salt and freshly ground black pepper, to taste

FISH

4 fillets Chilean sea bass, about 6 to 8 ounces each, 1½ inches thick

2 tablespoons unsalted butter

½ cup fish broth or water

Juice of 1 lemon (about 3 tablespoons)

½ teaspoon paprika

Preheat the oven to 450°F.

Toss the cubed eggplant with ¼ cup of the olive oil, place in a baking pan in one layer, and roast for 14 to 16 minutes, turning once. Reserve. Don't turn off the oven.

Heat the remaining ¼ cup oil in a large nonstick skillet over low flame and sauté the garlic for about 2 minutes, or until golden. Add the bell peppers, basil, anchovy fillets, capers, olives, parsley, and reserved eggplant. Stir to combine and sauté over low heat for 2 minutes. Add the tomatoes and ¾ cup water and bring to a boil. Cover, reduce the heat to low, and simmer for 12 minutes, or until the ingredients are thoroughly blended. Season with salt and pepper and keep warm on the lowest possible heat.

Place the fish in one layer in a baking dish and dot with butter. Pour the fish broth and lemon juice over and around the fish, and sprinkle with the paprika. Bake for 16 to 18 minutes, or until fish flakes easily with a fork.

To assemble, spoon two thirds of the sauce on a serving platter. Arrange the fish on top of the sauce, and spoon the remaining sauce over and around the fish.

Tony Bennett

I've been going to Patsy's for more than fifty years. We mostly ate at home when I was growing up, but when the family did go out it was to Patsy's—that's because my mother felt that food there was like home. And that meant we would be sure to like it.

"Later on, I went with Frank Sinatra and some of our musician friends. And when I perform in New York, I'm probably there twice a week. Recently, I was in New York to do some recordings, and I had Patsy's send food over for the whole crew at the studio every night that we were working. It's great Italian home-style cooking.

"Last year when Nancy Sinatra—Frank's daughter—and I were in New York working to establish the Frank Sinatra School of the Arts, the Scognamillos gave us a great send-off party at the restaurant. They must have served every dish they had on the menu, but I still have one favorite: Sal's Chilean Sea Bass. As far as I'm concerned, it's the best sea bass in New York City."

Jerry Stiller

"The first time Anne and I went to Patsy's was after we did the *Ed Sullivan Show* in the sixties. We went there to celebrate, and ever since when we go to Patsy's we feel like we're celebrating. I feel a real personal connection to Patsy's that goes beyond the food. It's like being part of the family. Patsy's has the best Italian food in the city—they cook things for you, ask how you want dishes prepared, and then they make them to order. And that's not just for us: I see them doing the same thing for all their guests.

"For me, Patsy's is more than food. I've gotten to know the Scognamillos, and the people who work there. The waiters make you feel important, but they do it without being haughty or presumptuous.

"You know, when you first come to New York, or first start in show busi-ness, you have an idea—a picture in your mind—of the New York style of life. Patsy's embodies that idea. Anne and I would take our kids there, Ben and Amy, it was part of our lives, and it still is.

"My favorite dishes? I think there is a real distinction to their fish. I'm a ple-beian, so I like pasta—anything made with garlic and oil."

CASSUOLA DI CALAMARI

CALAMARI IS A FAVORITE AT PATSY'S, BUT MANY OF OUR CUSTOMERS ARE afraid to prepare it at home because they think that cleaning squid is a big job. Well, it is. However, if your supermarket doesn't carry squid that has been cleaned and sliced, a solution is to ask your favorite fishmonger to clean the squid and cut it in to ¾-inch rings. After that, preparing squid is simple.

SERVES 4 TO 6

¼ cup olive oil

4 garlic cloves, minced

2 large yellow onions, chopped

2½ pounds cleaned squid, cut into
   ¾-inch rings

¼ cup fresh chopped basil

¼ cup fresh chopped flat-leaf parsley

¼ cup dry white wine

½ teaspoon crushed red pepper flakes

Salt and freshly ground black pepper,
   to taste

Heat the oil in a large skillet or Dutch oven over low flame and sauté the garlic for about 2 minutes, or until lightly browned. Add the onions, increase the heat slightly, cover, and simmer for 7 to 8 minutes, or until the onions are soft and translucent.

Meanwhile, bring 4 quarts of water to boil in a large pot. Reduce to a simmer and add the squid. Cook for 20 to 25 minutes, or until the squid is tender. Drain and add the squid to the garlic and onions. Stir in the basil, parsley, wine, red pepper flakes, salt and pepper to taste, and 1½ cups water. Bring to a boil, reduce the heat to a simmer, cover, and cook for 20 minutes, or until the ingredients are thoroughly blended, adding more water if necessary.

FILLET OF SOLE
ARREGANATA

THIS LIGHT DISH HAS ALWAYS BEEN VERY POPULAR ON OUR MENU. THERE are many ways to prepare sole, but I happen to like this style because the flavor of the fish comes through. You can use lemon sole or gray sole, but the most important thing is to buy only the freshest fish possible, never frozen.

SERVES 4

2½ pounds of lemon or gray sole
(about 8 fillets)

2 tablespoons unsalted butter

Juice of 1 lemon (about ¼ cup), plus
1 lemon for garnish

¼ cup white wine

½ teaspoon paprika

½ cup Seasoned Bread Crumbs
(see page 49)

¼ cup extra-virgin olive oil, for drizzling

Preheat the oven to 400°F.

Place the fish fillets in a baking dish and dot with butter. Combine the lemon juice and white wine in a small bowl, mix, and spoon over the fish. Season with paprika and roast for about 15 minutes, or until the fish flakes easily when tested with a fork.

Set the oven to broil. Put 1 tablespoon of seasoned bread crumbs on each fillet, drizzle with a little olive oil, and broil until lightly browned, about 2 minutes. Serve with lemon wedges.

Debbie Reynolds

"I was rehearsing for *Irene*, a Broadway show, when I first went to Patsy's. The family atmosphere made me and everyone so happy. I remember Patsy —his friendly smile, and the gray jacket he wore when he refilled the basket with that delicious bread. It was so great the way the whole family was there—the mother, the father, their kids. It was all so friendly and the food was delicious—those terrific tiny clams in that great red sauce! If I lived in New York, I'd be there two or three times a week."

TROTA
ALLA GIARDINO

HOW LONG SHOULD FISH BE COOKED? I KNOW A LOT OF CHEFS WHO SAY that fish should be cooked to medium rare. It looks great that way, translucent and kind of pearly. But if you talk to the health experts, they say that fish should be cooked thoroughly because many waters are impure and fish can harbor parasites and bacteria. What do I do? I cook fish until *just* done—overcook fish and it turns dry and tough. So how do you know when fish is just done? Give it the fork test: a fish steak or fillet should flake when gently pierced with a fork.

SERVES 4

8 large white mushrooms, cleaned and
   thinly sliced

1 medium red bell pepper, thinly sliced

4 fillets of sea trout (or striped bass),
   each 6 to 8 ounces

4 tablespoons unsalted butter

¼ cup lemon juice (about 1 medium
   lemon)

¼ cup plus 2 tablespoons olive oil

8 garlic cloves, thinly sliced

½ pound asparagus, washed, trimmed,
   and diagonally sliced into 1-inch
   pieces

1 10-ounce package frozen chopped
   spinach, cooked and drained

¼ cup dry white wine

Salt and freshly ground black pepper,
   to taste

½ cup Seasoned Bread Crumbs (page 49)

2 tablespoons chopped fresh flat-leaf
   parsley

Bring a large pot of water to a boil, add the mushrooms and bell pepper, and blanch for 2 minutes. Drain and reserve.

Preheat the oven to 450°F.

Place the fish fillets in a single layer in a baking pan, dot with 2 tablespoons of the butter, and sprinkle with the lemon juice. Roast for 14 to 16 minutes, or until fish flakes easily when tested with a fork. Remove from the oven and reserve.

Meanwhile, heat ¼ cup of the olive oil in a large nonstick skillet over low flame and sauté the garlic until lightly browned, about 2 minutes. Add the blanched mushrooms and bell pepper, the asparagus, spinach, and the remaining 2 tablespoons of butter. Increase the heat to medium and sauté the vegetables for 2 minutes, stirring occasionally. Add the wine and ½ cup water to the skillet, cover, and cook for about 5 minutes, or until most of the liquid has evaporated and the asparagus is crisp-tender. Season to taste with salt and pepper.

Spread the vegetables on the bottom of an ovenproof serving platter and arrange the cooked fish fillets on top. Spread the bread crumbs over the fish and drizzle with the remaining 2 tablespoons olive oil. Bake for an additional 4 to 5 minutes, or until all ingredients are heated through and the bread crumbs are lightly browned.

Mrs. Sammy Davis Jr.

"I've always loved going to Patsy's, because whether I was there with Sammy, without Sammy, or at Patsy's since Sammy passed away, I am always treated with respect," says Altovise Davis. "They're all gentlemen at Patsy's—Joe and Sal and Frank, everyone who works there. I'm there often with women friends, and you know how some restaurants treat women—not great. But a woman who goes to Patsy's doesn't have to fret if she doesn't have a male escort.

"Whenever I would come in from the coast, I would go to Patsy's to see the family. Sammy was there a lot—he often took people to Patsy's. I remember once when we were there with our son Manny, who was about ten, and Frank taught him how to eat spaghetti. 'Don't use a spoon,' he said, 'you've got to learn to twirl it!' And so Manny learned the right way to eat spaghetti. We always have good times at Patsy's."

ROASTED STRIPED BASS
WITH HORSERADISH CRUST

THIS IS ANOTHER DISH THAT WAS REQUESTED BY MY CUSTOMERS. IT SEEMS that fish coated with horseradish is popular, and I always do my best to honor requests. Horseradish also works well with other fish, and salmon steaks may be substituted for the striped bass.

SERVES 4

4 fillets of striped bass, each 6 to 8 ounces, skin removed

2 tablespoons unsalted butter

¼ cup lemon juice (about 1 lemon)

¼ cup fish broth or water

¼ teaspoon paprika

¼ teaspoon salt

¼ teaspoon freshly ground black pepper

3 scallions (white and green parts), finely sliced

4 tablespoons horseradish, drained

4 tablespoons Dijon mustard

2 tablespoons mayonnaise

1 tablespoon dry bread crumbs

Preheat the oven to 400°F.

Place the fish fillets in a baking dish and dot with the butter. Combine the lemon juice and broth in a small bowl, mix, and spoon over the fish. Season with the paprika, salt, and pepper, and roast for about 20 minutes, or until the fish flakes easily when tested with a fork.

Meanwhile, combine the scallions, horseradish, mustard, mayonnaise, and bread crumbs in a bowl. Mix thoroughly.

Turn the oven to broil. Spread the horseradish mixture over the fish and broil until the crust is lightly browned, about 2 minutes.

QUICK AND EASY
Lobster Fra Diavolo

We get a lot of interesting calls and requests from our customers, especially at dinner time, and often on weekends. One such call came from a customer who had been dining at Patsy's for years. She had been brought to the restaurant by her parents, who had been brought to the restaurant by her grandparents. You might say we have a relationship.

Her call came from Southampton, Long Island, on a Saturday afternoon. "Sal," she said, "I have weekend guests, and you know what they brought as a house gift? Four cooked lobsters. I could serve them cold or in a salad, but I'd like to do something more interesting. Any ideas? And make it simple."

"That's easy," I said. "Do you have a couple of jars of our Fra Diavolo Sauce?"

"Are you kidding? I have all your sauces. Are you saying I could make a Lobster Fra Diavolo? What do I do?"

"First, split the lobsters. Can you do that?"

"No. But my husband can."

"Okay. Do you have a really large skillet, or maybe a big saucepan?"

"I'll look. I must have."

"Then empty 4 cups of Patsy's Fra Diavolo sauce into the skillet. Bring it to a boil and add ½ cup dry wine, and ¼ cup chopped fresh flat-leaf parsley. Reduce the heat and let it simmer for 10 minutes. Turn off the heat until you're ready to eat.

"When it's dinner time, heat the sauce. Place a lobster on each plate and top it with sauce. If you really want to do it Patsy's style, cook up linguine to serve with the lobster and spoon sauce over the pasta, too."

PATSY MEETS *Dalí and Picasso*

"Many famous artists have dined at Patsy's," says Joe. "Salvador Dalí was a frequent visitor, usually accompanied by a gorgeous model, such as Carmen. One evening he arrived with a book he had written, part art, part cookbook, and signed it with a dedication to my father. Then there was the time when one of the waiters came into the kitchen, very excited, to tell me that Pablo Picasso and a party of friends had arrived. I looked out through the kitchen door, and there he was—the greatest artist of the twentieth century—having dinner at Patsy's.

"It was a wonderful night for us, and I remember that we sent out course after course to Picasso's table. A sensualist about food as well as about women, Picasso ate every dish with gusto and sent compliments back to the kitchen, especially, he said, for the Lobster Fra Diavolo.

"If I was excited to have him there, my father was calm as usual, wearing his gray jacket, moving quietly among the tables, making sure that all our guests were being properly served.

"That was the first time that Picasso came to Patsy's, but not the last. He would visit us whenever he came to New York, and he always ordered at least one dish with our Fra Diavolo Sauce. He got to know our family, and some of the awe I felt was replaced by a warmer feeling of friendship. One late evening after Picasso and his friends had left the restaurant and we were doing a final cleanup before closing, my father told me that Picasso had so enjoyed his dinner that he said he wanted to give my father one of his paintings.

"A genuine Picasso—I was overwhelmed. I asked my father when we could expect the painting. My father just shrugged and said, 'I thanked him, of course, but I said that I couldn't accept such an expensive gift.'

"'Why? Why did you do that?'

"My father's eyebrows went up. 'Have you seen his paintings, Joe? An eye at one angle, a nose beneath the chin, the face all mixed up. A nice man, Picasso, but no Michelangelo, no Raphael.'

"I groaned, but there was no arguing with my father. The next time Pablo Picasso came to Patsy's he brought us a gift. Not a painting, but a beautiful art book with photographs of his work. A wonderful gesture, but I would rather have had the painting."

PROSCIUTTO-WRAPPED MONKFISH

I THINK MONKFISH IS DELICIOUS AND NEEDS NO EXPLANATION, BUT monkfish has been called the "poor man's lobster." When I heard that name, I decided to prepare monkfish to imitate the look of lobster meat. I wrapped prosciutto around the fish, and as it roasts the prosciutto tightens around the fish, creating the look of lobster—an appealing fool-the-eye effect.

SERVES 4

½ teaspoon crushed red pepper flakes

⅔ cup Seasoned Bread Crumbs (page 49)

4 monkfish fillets (about 6 ounces each)

Salt and freshly ground black pepper, to
   taste

4 basil leaves

4 thin slices prosciutto (about ⅛ pound)

1 tablespoon unsalted butter, for coating
   dish

Juice of 1 lemon (about 2 to
   3 tablespoons)

¼ cup white wine

Preheat the oven to 450°F.

In a small bowl, combine the red pepper flakes and the bread crumbs, and mix thoroughly.

Season the fish fillets with salt and pepper, and coat in the bread crumbs. On the top of each piece of fish place a basil leaf, and wrap a slice of prosciutto around the fillets, securing with a toothpick (prosciutto tends to curl when baking). The fish now resembles a lobster tail.

Coat a shallow baking dish with the butter, and add the lemon juice and white wine. Place the fish in the pan and roast for 18 to 22 minutes, or until fish flakes easily when tested with a fork. Transfer the fish to a serving platter and spoon over the pan juices.

My Grandfather
AND HIS GRAY JACKET

A number of our customers who have been coming to Patsy's for many years have commented that my grandfather always wore a gray cotton jacket, and looked like a busboy or an unassuming waiter. He said that he didn't want the customers to know he was the owner because then they would feel diffident about asking him for a glass of water. And he also wanted to feel free to pitch in—clean a table, refill a breadbasket. Restaurant owners don't usually do things like that.

That was his style, and everyone respected him for it. My father tells me that when the restaurant was giving a party to celebrate its twenty-fifth anniversary, everyone in the family who worked at the restaurant decided to get really dressed up for the event. My father ordered a new tuxedo, as did my cousin, Frank.

"When are you going to the tailor to order your tuxedo?" my father asked Patsy.

"No tuxedo for me," said my grandfather. "I'll be at the party same as always, in my gray jacket."

"But Pa," my father said, "this is a special occasion!"

"You want to see me there?" asked my grandfather. "Then you'll see me in my gray jacket."

And that's how it was. My father, Frank, and some of our customers wore tuxedos. My grandfather was in his gray jacket. And as my father says, he was the most elegant man there.

SALMON WITH HERB SAUCE

SALMON HAS LONG BEEN A FAVORITE FISH AT PATSY'S, AND LOOKING FOR a slightly different presentation and an unusual flavor, I created a version that incorporates a variety of tastes.

SERVES 4

3 tablespoons mayonnaise

1 tablespoon minced fresh flat-leaf parsley

1 scallion (white and green parts), minced

1 tablespoon nonpareil capers, rinsed, drained, and chopped

4 center-cut salmon fillets (10 ounces each)

2 tablespoons unsalted butter, at room temperature

Salt and freshly ground black pepper

Paprika, to taste

1/8 cup clam juice or broth

Juice of 1 lemon, plus 1 whole lemon, cut into 8 wedges

Preheat the oven to 450°F.

In a small mixing bowl, combine the mayonnaise, parsley, scallion, and capers. Mix thoroughly, cover, and reserve.

Arrange the salmon fillets in an 8 × 10 × 2-inch baking dish. Dot the fish with the butter and sprinkle with salt, pepper, and paprika. Pour the clam juice and lemon juice over and around the fish, and bake in the preheated oven for 16 to 18 minutes, or until the fish flakes easily when fork-tested.

Remove from the oven and turn on the broiler. Spread a thin layer of the reserved mayonnaise mixture on each fillet, and broil for 2 minutes, or until lightly browned. Remove the fillets from the baking dish with a slotted spatula and arrange on a serving platter with the lemon wedges.

SAUTÉED
SHRIMP WITH COGNAC AND DIJON MUSTARD

THERE ARE SO MANY THINGS TO DO WITH SHRIMP THAT THEIR VERY presence suggests new recipes. Here's one that I developed as I was experimenting in my kitchen one night after the restaurant had closed. No, it's not Neapolitan, but it has become a favorite with some of my customers from Milan who come to New York for Fashion Week.

SERVES 4

24 jumbo shrimp (about 1½ pounds), peeled, deveined, and rinsed
½ cup all-purpose flour
¼ cup olive oil
1 tablespoon unsalted butter
6 scallions (white and green parts), thinly sliced

1 cup chicken broth
¼ cup chopped fresh flat-leaf parsley
⅓ cup Cognac
¼ cup dry white wine
2 tablespoons Dijon mustard
Salt and freshly ground black pepper, to taste

Coat the shrimp with the flour. Heat the oil in a large nonstick skillet over medium flame and sauté the shrimp for 2 minutes. Remove the shrimp (they will not be cooked through at this point) and reserve.

Remove the oil from the skillet and discard. Add the butter and the scallions to the skillet and sauté over low heat, stirring, for 3 minutes. Add the broth, return the partially cooked shrimp, and simmer for additional 2 minutes. Add the parsley, Cognac, wine, and mustard. Stir to combine, cover, and continue to simmer over low heat for 4 minutes, or until the shrimp are cooked through. Season to taste with salt and pepper.

Helen Gurley Brown

"No one brought me to Patsy's. It turned out to be very much in the neighborhood of my new job, editor of *Cosmopolitan* magazine, which I began in l965. I don't remember my first meal, but I do remember the friendliness of what seemed to be a warm, Italian family. The maître d', the captain, the waiter, somebody checking coats were all friendly.

"My fondest memories of the restaurant are all the quiet, delicious dinners with David Brown, my husband, maybe before or after a movie, occasionally because mother just didn't feel like going home after work and cooking.

"I do remember a rollicking evening Rosie Clooney gave for her birthday—or somebody gave it for her—that was l999. Upstairs a lot of twinkly people like Tony Bennett were there, but it was a family kind of evening. Many of her children were there.

"My favorite meal at Patsy's? One of their great shrimp dishes, and I know that if I want something that's not on the menu, Joe or Sal will be happy to prepare it for me."

CALAMARI SALAD

FRIED CALAMARI IS A GREAT, CRUNCHY FAVORITE. BUT FOR A LIGHTER DISH, I prefer a calamari salad. Prepared with a dressing, and tossed with a few vegetables, Calamari Salad can be served either as an appetizer or as a main luncheon course.

SERVES 4

2 pounds cleaned calamari, cut into
   ½-inch rings
¼ cup olive oil
Juice of 2 lemons
2 ribs celery, cut into ½-inch slices

20 gaeta or kalamata olives, pits removed
1 garlic clove, minced
2 tablespoons finely minced fresh basil
Salt and freshly ground black pepper,
   to taste

Bring a large pot of water to a boil and cook the calamari rings for 20 to 25 minutes or until tender. Drain and place in cold water to cool for 15 to 30 minutes. Drain and reserve.

In a large bowl, combine the oil, lemon juice, celery, olives, garlic, and basil. Add the cooled calamari rings and mix thoroughly. Season to taste with salt and pepper, and refrigerate for at least 1 hour to infuse the flavors. Serve chilled or at room temperature.

SHRIMP
MILANESE

½ cup all-purpose flour

3 large eggs, lightly beaten

1 cup Seasoned Bread Crumbs (page 49)

1½ pounds large or extra-large shrimp
(about 24), peeled, deveined, and
rinsed

1 cup olive oil

Salt and freshly ground black pepper, to
taste

1 lemon, cut into wedges, for garnish

Put the flour on a large plate, the beaten eggs in a shallow bowl, and the bread crumbs on another large plate. Lightly coat the shrimp in the flour, then the beaten eggs, and then the bread crumbs.

Heat the oil in a large skillet to a frying temperature of 375°F. Fry the shrimp (in batches, if necessary), turning once, for 4 minutes, or until cooked through. Drain on paper towels. Season with salt and pepper, and serve with lemon wedges.

SHRIMP SCAMPI

AS EVERYONE KNOWS BY NOW, *SCAMPI* IS SYNONYMOUS WITH SHRIMP IN Italian restaurants, but Shrimp Scampi has come to mean shrimp prepared to a sizzle with butter and plenty of garlic. It's so simple to prepare, and so rich with flavor, that it's easy to see why it's a perennial favorite.

SERVES 4

3 tablespoons unsalted butter

6 garlic cloves, minced

16 jumbo shrimp (about 1½ pounds),
    peeled and deveined

Juice of 2 lemons

½ cup clam juice or broth

Dash of Worcestershire sauce

½ teaspoon paprika

¼ cup Seasoned Bread Crumbs (page 49)

2 tablespoons olive oil

Salt and freshly ground black pepper,
    to taste

Preheat the broiler.

Heat the butter in an ovenproof skillet over low flame and sauté the garlic until lightly golden, about 2 to 3 minutes. Add the shrimp and continue to cook for 1 to 2 minutes, or until the shrimp are coated with the garlic butter. Add the lemon juice, clam juice, and Worcestershire sauce, and bring to a boil. Cover, reduce the heat to low, and simmer for 1 to 2 minutes.

Uncover the skillet, sprinkle the shrimp with the paprika, and place under the broiler for 5 to 6 minutes, or until the shrimp are lightly browned and cooked through. Remove the skillet, top the mixture with the bread crumbs, drizzle with the oil, and return to the broiler for 2 minutes, or until the bread crumbs are lightly browned.

Anna ON FILM

"Everyone comes to Patsy's. Part of *Raging Bull* was written at the bar. And Jake LaMotta and his wife, Vicki, would have dinner here with Robert De Niro. Mario Puzo had us in his book *The Godfather*. The scene where Luca Brasi was killed was supposed to have happened at Patsy's. You'll find us in the book on page 109. Directors love atmosphere, and when *The Godfather* movie was being filmed they wanted to shoot that scene here. But my father said no. He hated violence, and he said he didn't want his customers to think of that bloody scene when they were eating dinner. Of course, today with so many popular TV shows and movies about the Mafia, he might have felt differently. Mario Puzo was here all the time, and Joe DiMaggio came almost every night with his first wife and son.

"Dustin Hoffman came here to meet Arthur Miller, and he wasn't wearing a jacket so I brought him one of our house jackets. He kind of hesitated, so I said, 'I can bring you a gown if you prefer—it was when he was appearing in *Tootsie*. He put the jacket on and signed the contract to do *Death of a Salesman* while he was sitting here."

"*I* came to Patsy's in 1964 when I first moved to New York, and I've been dining there ever since."

—SOUPY SALES

SWORDFISH STEAKS
ARREGANATA

SWORDFISH IS A GREAT, MEATY FISH. THE PREPARATION IS SIMPLE: JUST treat a swordfish steak the way you would a beef steak. I suggest serving it with the same sides you would use for a porterhouse: spinach and sliced tomatoes and onions.

SERVES 4

4 swordfish steaks, each 6 to 8 ounces

Salt and freshly ground black pepper,
   to taste

1 tablespoon unsalted butter

¼ cup lemon juice

Paprika, to taste

1 cup Seasoned Bread Crumbs (page 49)

3 tablespoons olive oil

Preheat the oven to 450°F.

Place the fish in a shallow roasting pan. Season with the salt and pepper, dot with the butter, spoon over the lemon juice, and sprinkle with the paprika.

Add ¼ cup water to the pan and roast the fish for 15 to 17 minutes, or until it flakes easily when tested with a fork.

Remove from the oven and turn on broiler. Spread 2 tablespoons of the bread crumbs over each fish steak, and drizzle with the olive oil. Broil for 2 to 3 minutes, or until the crumbs are lightly browned.

Joe Piscopo GOES FOR AMBIANCE

"The family is always front and center, and they make you feel welcome and comfortable, and the clientele is hip enough not to stare at celebrities when they come in. I was there shortly after Frank Sinatra died, and it was moving to listen to the Scognamillo family tell Frank stories. You could just feel Francis Albert there, hangin' with his cronies."

MARINATED
TUNA STEAKS
WITH CILANTRO SAUCE

HERE'S PROOF THAT TUNA DOES NOT HAVE TO COME FROM A CAN. THE secret here is not to overcook the fish.

SERVE 4

7 garlic cloves, 1 finely minced and 6
   thinly sliced

2 tablespoons mayonnaise

1 tablespoon lemon juice

2 tablespoons chopped fresh cilantro

4 tuna steaks, each 6 to 8 ounces

Salt and freshly ground black pepper,
   to taste

⅓ cup olive oil

Pinch of oregano

In a small bowl, mix the minced garlic, mayonnaise, lemon juice, and cilantro. Cover and refrigerate.

Sprinkle the tuna with the salt and pepper. In a dish, combine the oil, sliced garlic, and oregano. Mix. Add the tuna steaks, turning several times so that both sides are coated with the oil. Cover the dish and refrigerate, allowing the steaks to marinate for 2 to 3 hours. Remove the dish 15 minutes before preheating the broiler, and allow to warm slightly.

Preheat the broiler.

Remove the tuna from the dish, discarding the marinade. Arrange the fish on a broiler pan and broil for about 3 to 4 minutes, or until medium rare. Spoon the cilantro mixture on the top of each steak and continue to broil for 1 to 2 minutes, or until the sauce has lightly browned.

8

ITALIANS TRADITIONALLY PREFER FRESH FRUIT FOR DESSERT, and even many of their cooked desserts are made with fruit. You'll find recipes here for poached figs and pears, as well as desserts that are more festive, such as Warm Chocolate Cake, a sweet delight, especially when served with a dollop of whipped cream. For a light sweet, baked maddalena cookies are a wonderful addition to an assortment of fresh fruit.

Some much-beloved Italian desserts, such as Pasticiotto or Sfogliatelle, are probably best obtained from a fine Italian bakery. We can prepare them in our restaurant, but they are awfully difficult to make at home.

DESSERTS

MICHELE'S CHEESECAKE

WARM CHOCOLATE CAKE

CHOCOLATE MOUSSE

TIRAMISÙ

MADDALENA RASPBERRY COOKIES

LEMON GRANITA

COFFEE GRANITA WITH WHIPPED CREAM

FRESH FIGS POACHED WITH VANILLA
    AND BRANDY

MACEDOINE OF ORANGES WITH SAMBUCA

PEACHES IN ASTI SPUMANTE

PEARS POACHED WITH PEAR LIQUEUR

LEMON RICOTTA TORTE

ZABAGLIONE

WALNUT-FILLED CREPES

MICHELE'S CHEESECAKE

MICHELE HAS BEEN WORKING IN OUR RESTAURANT'S OFFICE FOR TWENTY years. If you're one of our customers, you've seen her—she's the tall, pretty blonde who comes running down the stairs, usually with a pad and some papers that she says either I or my father have to look at immediately. She's a part of the Patsy's family, and it's her cheesecake that we all enjoy when any of us has a birthday, anniversary, or anything else wonderful to celebrate. Michele makes the cake at home with loving care, and brings it in appropriately decorated, with a box of tiny candles to add the final touch.

This is an all-American cheesecake, and you won't find it on our menu. But Michele and her cake are special to us, so we're including it in our book. And if you should be at Patsy's when Michele's cake is being served, I'm sure that she'll offer you a taste.

SERVES 12 TO 14

CRUST	FILLING
⅓ cup butter (about 5 tablespoons)	1 pound cream cheese, softened
1¼ cups graham cracker crumbs	1 cup sugar
¼ cup sugar	3 large eggs
	1 pint sour cream
	1 tablespoon vanilla extract

Preheat the oven to 375°F.

In a small saucepan, melt the butter over low flame. In a medium mixing bowl, combine the graham cracker crumbs, sugar, and melted butter and mix until thoroughly combined. Transfer the crumb mixture to an 8-inch springform pan; using the back of a spoon, press the crumbs against the bottom and sides of the pan. Place in the oven and bake for 6 to 8 minutes, or until the crust is lightly browned. Remove from the oven and allow to cool before filling.

Reduce the oven temperature to 350°F.

In a large mixing bowl, combine the cream cheese and sugar, and mix. Add the eggs, one at a time, and continue mixing. Stir in the sour cream and the vanilla and mix until thoroughly blended. Spoon the cheese mixture into the crust. Smooth the top with a spatula.

Bake for 30 minutes. Turn off the oven and allow the cake to remain in the oven for an additional hour, then remove and allow to cool. Refrigerate for at least 6 hours, preferably overnight, before serving.

To serve, slide a knife around the side of the cake to separate it from the pan. Release the pan's spring and carefully remove.

Michael Feinstein

"I was first introduced to Patsy's by my 'Beverly Hills Mom,' Rosemary Clooney. I immediately felt at home. Everyone who works there seems proud to be part of the restaurant. It's good to know that in a rapidly changing world, Patsy's is one place where you can count on good food and a great welcome. Everybody goes to Patsy's, and I remember a special night when I introduced Liza Minnelli to the great songwriter Irving Caesar. He gave us an impromptu concert of some of his hits, 'Swanee' and 'Tea for Two.'

"I love Patsy's Chicken Sausages in Marinara Sauce. But the night Joey introduced me to Frank Sinatra's favorite dessert, Pasticiotto, was really a peak experience. I've given Patsy's sauces to friends, and when they prepare a meal for me with one of the sauces, it's almost as though I were back in the restaurant. So good! I travel a lot, and when I get back to New York and walk into Patsy's, the welcome I get from Joey makes me wish I were Italian! (Don't tell my parents I said that.)"

WARM
CHOCOLATE CAKE

THESE INDIVIDUAL CHOCOLATE CAKES, WITH A SOFT CENTER AND SERVED while still warm, are irresistible. They're great by themselves, but served with fresh strawberries and a heaping spoonful of whipped cream, they're even better.

SERVES 4

2 tablespoons unsalted butter, plus
    more for coating ramekins
4 tablespoons all-purpose flour, sifted,
    plus more for coating ramekins
11 ounces bittersweet chocolate
    (66% cocoa)
2 tablespoons sugar

1 ounce coffee-flavored liqueur
    (such as Kahlúa)
Pinch of salt
1 large egg
1 egg yolk
Confectioners' sugar, for dusting
1 cup sliced fresh strawberries (optional)
½ pint heavy cream, whipped (optional)

Preheat the oven to 350°F.

Lightly coat four 4-ounce disposable foil dessert cups with butter and flour. Shake out excess flour and reserve.

In the top of a double boiler, combine the chocolate, 2 tablespoons of butter, sugar, coffee-flavored liqueur, and salt. Cook over gently simmering hot water, stirring, until the chocolate has melted and all the ingredients are combined.

Remove from the heat and slowly beat in the whole egg and egg yolk. Stir in the 4 tablespoons of flour, 1 tablespoon at a time, until the chocolate mixture is thoroughly blended. Divide the batter equally among the prepared dessert cups.

Bake for 11 to 13 minutes (check after 11 minutes). The top should look baked on the outer edges and moist in a quarter-size center. Remove from the oven and allow to cool for 10 to 20 minutes. Invert the dessert cups over 4 individual dessert plates, and tap gently on the top and sides until the cakes slide out onto the plates. The cakes will be warm and soft in the center. Dust with the confectioners' sugar, spoon the strawberries and whipped cream beside the cakes (if using), and serve immediately.

COMEDIAN *Dick Capri*

"The first time I went to Patsy's, I was sitting and eating their great Spaghetti Marinara. And two of my favorite idols walked by: Frank Sinatra and Dean Martin. Everyone at the restaurant looked up from their meal to stare at these two great legends. I also wanted to look up, but I couldn't get my face out of the plate of delicious pasta.

"Now I have three idols!"

"I head for Patsy's Restaurant whenever I'm in New York. I enjoy both the southern Italian home cooking and the warm welcome that greets me. Joe and Anna always ask about my kids, and that makes me feel like part of the Scognamillo family."

—GREGORY PECK

CHOCOLATE MOUSSE

THIS IS A MOUSSE I DEVELOPED ONE NIGHT IN OUR KITCHEN WHEN THE restaurant was closed—that's when I do some of my best work. I prepare it with a coffee-flavored liqueur, but it would also be fine with an orange liqueur such as Grand Marnier or Cointreau.

SERVES 4 TO 6

1¾ cups heavy cream

½ teaspoon vanilla extract

2 tablespoons confectioners' sugar

1¼ cups (10 ounces) semisweet chocolate morsels

2 tablespoons coffee-flavored liqueur (such as Kahlúa or Tia Maria)

2 tablespoons brewed espresso

1 tablespoon unsalted butter, softened at room temperature

1 tablespoon granulated sugar

1 extra-large egg

Combine the cream, vanilla, and sugar in a large, deep bowl. Using an electric mixer or a hand beater, whip until soft peaks are formed. Refrigerate and reserve.

In the top of a double boiler, combine the chocolate morsels, coffee-flavored liqueur, espresso, butter, and granulated sugar. Cook over gently simmering hot water, stirring, just until the chocolate has melted and all the ingredients are combined. Remove from the heat.

Whip the egg in the top of a double boiler until foamy and fold into the chocolate mixture. Gently fold the reserved whipped cream into the mixture. Spoon into a serving bowl, or dessert dishes, and refrigerate for 4 hours, or until chilled and set.

TIRAMISÙ

THIS POPULAR DESSERT IS SO RICH THAT I PREFER SERVING IT AT HOME ON a Sunday afternoon when friends and family come by to gossip over cups of good strong coffee. Of course you can serve it at the end of a meal, but make sure that the meal is a light one. Ladyfingers may be purchased at many Italian bakeries.

SERVES 6 TO 8

4 large eggs, separated	2 to 4 tablespoons Cognac
1 pint heavy cream	20 to 24 ladyfingers
$2/3$ cup plus 2 tablespoons sugar	1½ cups brewed espresso, chilled
8 ounces mascarpone	1 tablespoon cocoa

Place egg whites in top of a double boiler and beat over simmering water until the whites form soft peaks.

Place egg yolks in top of another double boiler and beat until the yolks are thick and lemon-colored and reach a temperature of 160°F. Reserve.

Whip the cream until soft peaks are formed. Reserve.

In a large mixing bowl, combine the $2/3$ cup sugar, mascarpone, and Cognac, and beat for 2 to 3 minutes, or until smooth. Gently fold the reserved egg yolks into the mascarpone mixture, followed by the reserved egg whites and the reserved whipped cream, until all the ingredients are thoroughly blended.

Pour the espresso in a small bowl. Dip each ladyfinger in the espresso, and layer them in the bottom and sides of a large glass bowl. Top with ½ of the mascarpone mixture, add a middle layer of espresso-dipped ladyfingers, and spread the remaining mascarpone mixture on top. Sprinkle with cocoa. Refrigerate 1 hour before serving.

MADDALENA
RASPBERRY COOKIES

FRANCE HAS ITS MADELEINE COOKIES, MADE FAMOUS BY MARCEL PROUST, and Italy has its maddalena cookies, not as well known. Which came first? According to the Italians, an Italian queen married a French king and was responsible for taking the knowledge of fine food to France. I'm not going to argue this one, but I do recommend our maddalena cookies, which are wonderful with espresso or a small glass of sweet dessert wine.

MAKES 20 COOKIES

½ pound unsalted butter	2 large eggs
2¾ cups all-purpose flour	2 egg yolks
1 cup sugar	½ cup milk
Pinch of baking powder	¾ cup raspberry preserves
Pinch of salt	Confectioners' sugar, for dusting

Preheat the oven to 325°F.

In a small saucepan, melt the butter over low heat. Set aside.

In an electric mixer fitted with a paddle whisk, combine the flour, sugar, baking powder, and salt. Mix at low speed until ingredients are blended.

With the mixer running at low speed, add the melted butter gradually, and continue beating for 2 minutes. Add the eggs and yolks, one at a time, until all the ingredients are combined. Continue beating for 1 minute. Add the milk and continue beating at a higher speed until the dough is smooth and pliable.

Fit a pastry bag with ½-inch-diameter open-star tip and fill two-thirds full with dough. Pipe onto a nonstick baking sheet or parchment paper, creating rectangles approximately 3 × 1½ inches. Bake on the oven's middle shelf for 20 minutes. Remove and allow the cookies to cool.

When the cookies are cool enough to handle, spread each one with a thin layer of raspberry preserves. Press together two cookies, creating a sandwich. Dust with confectioners' sugar before serving.

Liz Smith

"My memories of Patsy's Restaurant are entirely fond. I get all warm and soppy just thinking about going there for dinner, because it's very much like going home back in the days when we actually liked going home. And always there was the glamour aura surrounding Patsy's because it was Frank Sinatra's favorite.

"Patsy's was—and is—an old-style, friendly, big, expansive, and overly generous kind of place. In an era now when restaurants are smart, pared-down, noisy, and full of people screaming, I still prefer the old-fashioned love and affection at Patsy's. Not that Patsy's is always quiet—those great big platters do make a lot of noise when they set them down. And then Patsy's is still a lure for celebrities and VIPs, so you always run into someone interesting.

"Maybe it's because I was born in Texas that I love Patsy's. I've always thought there was some connection between Texans and Italians. And Italy remains my favorite country outside the U.S. of A."

"A lot of big names have made Patsy's their second home. Of course, I'm just a little name, but they let me eat there anyway—thanks, guys!" —PAT COOPER

LEMON GRANITA

A GRANITA IS A LIGHT, FROZEN DESSERT MUCH LOVED IN ITALY. IT'S NOT AS rich as ice cream or gelato, and makes a perfect ending to a three- or four-course dinner—sweet and flavorful, but not too rich or filling.

SERVES 6

1 cup sugar

1 tablespoon grated fresh lemon peel

⅔ cup lemon juice (about 2 large lemons)

Dash of salt

In a large saucepan, combine the sugar with 4 cups water. Bring to a boil, stirring occasionally to dissolve sugar. Cool to room temperature. Add the lemon peel, lemon juice, and salt. Stir to combine.

Remove the grids from 2 metal ice cube trays (a 13 × 9 × 2-inch baking pan may be substituted for the ice cube trays). Pour the lemon mixture into the trays and place them in the freezer. Stir the mixture every 15 minutes. The mixture should become mushy, but not frozen solid. The granita will be ready to serve in about 3 hours.

JOE SAYS HELLO TO C. Everett Koop

I remember when C. Everett Koop was Surgeon General. He practically started the crusade to stop smoking. He came into the restaurant one day. I tried to get to my father, who was at the door, before he could ask the usual questions: "Would you like to sit upstairs or downstairs? Smoking or nonsmoking?" Those were the days when a smoking section was allowed in a New York restaurant. I could see by Dr. Koop's face that I hadn't gotten there soon enough—he was glaring at my father. I guess he didn't realize that my father hadn't recognized him, and he thought Dad was making fun of him. When I finally got to them, I said, "Dad, this is Dr. Koop. We've been reading a lot about him lately." My father did a double take, recovered his cool, and said, "Dr. Koop, let me take you upstairs to our nonsmoking room."

COFFEE
GRANITA WITH WHIPPED CREAM

CAN YOU MAKE ESPRESSO IF YOU DON'T OWN AN ESPRESSO MACHINE? Yes, you can. The secret is in the coffee. Purchase dark espresso coffee beans—if you have a coffee grinder, so much the better—and grind the beans just before preparing the coffee. If you don't have a grinder, have the beans ground where you purchase the coffee. But avoid buying ready-ground coffee, if you can. Much of the strength of the coffee will be lost while sitting on a supermarket shelf. Once you have your freshly ground espresso coffee, proceed to make coffee just the way you would at any other time. You'll see, this does work.

SERVES 6

2 cups strong espresso coffee   **½ pint heavy cream**

1 cup plus 3 teaspoons sugar

In a large saucepan, combine the coffee and 1 cup of sugar with 2 cups water. Bring to a boil and cook, stirring occasionally to dissolve sugar.

Remove the grids from 2 metal ice cube trays (a 13 × 9 × 2-inch baking pan may be substituted for the ice cube trays). Pour the coffee mixture into trays and place in the freezer. Stir the mixture every 15 minutes. The mixture should become mushy, but not frozen solid. The granita will be ready to serve in about 3 hours.

Place heavy cream in a mixing bowl. Add the 3 teaspoons sugar. Using an egg beater, whip the cream until thick.

Spoon the granita into dessert dishes and top with a dollop of whipped cream.

FRESH FIGS POACHED
WITH VANILLA AND BRANDY

ITALIANS LOVE FIGS—FRESH, POACHED, COMBINED WITH PROSCIUTTO OR cheese. No real Italian has ever met a fig he did not like. Coming to the United States, many Italian immigrants who lived in Brooklyn brownstones planted fig trees in the backyard.

This dish is prepared with figs that are just starting to ripen; a too-ripe fig would fall apart when poached.

SERVES 4

12 to 16 fresh figs, green or black,
    medium ripe

¼ cup sugar

¼ teaspoon vanilla extract

¼ cup brandy

2 tablespoons dark rum

Trim the bottom and top of each fig. Rinse fruit gently and place in a large saucepan.

Combine the sugar, ¾ cup water, and vanilla in a small bowl and mix. Pour over the figs and bring to a boil. Cover, reduce the heat to low, and allow figs to poach in simmering liquid for 3 minutes. Stir in the brandy and the rum, and poach for an additional 2 minutes. Using a slotted spoon, remove the figs from the liquid and reserve.

Bring the poaching liquid to a boil and cook for about 4 to 5 minutes, or until the liquid is reduced to a thin syrup. Allow the liquid to cool and pour over figs. Serve warm or at room temperature.

MACEDOINE OF ORANGES
WITH SAMBUCA

THIS IS ONE OF THE MOST REFRESHING OF ITALIAN DESSERTS. IF YOU WISH, you can eliminate the liqueur, or add another favorite flavor to replace the sambuca.

SERVES 4 TO 6

6 oranges (mineola, navel, temple, or
  blood oranges)

1 cup sugar

¼ cup sambuca (or anisette) liqueur

Peel the oranges and slice each horizontally, removing any seeds. Place the orange slices, overlapping slightly, on a serving platter.

Combine the sugar with ½ cup water in a small saucepan. Cook over low heat, stirring constantly until sugar dissolves. Add the sambuca and continue cooking, stirring occasionally, for 10 minutes.

Pour the syrup over the orange slices and refrigerate until chilled. Turn the orange slices in syrup occasionally. This dessert may be prepared up to 6 hours in advance.

JOE REMEMBERS *The Silver Dollars*

"My father's first restaurant was on West Forty-ninth Street," Joe recalls, "and then he opened Patsy's on West Fifty-sixth Street. A short time later, he bought an old building next door and had it torn down so he could build the restaurant we're in now. (Ahmet Ertegun and Atlantic Records had offices in the old building.) My father designed two kitchens: one downstairs and one upstairs. He was afraid that food would get cold if it had to be carried upstairs from a kitchen on the first floor. My father thought of everything.

"The man who built this restaurant was Jack Stern. After the restaurant was built, he said to my father, 'Don't worry about a thing, Patsy. I put a bunch of silver dollars in the foundation for good luck, and that means that Patsy's Restaurant will always make money.'"

PEACHES
IN ASTI SPUMANTE

"WHEN MY FATHER FIRST OPENED PATSY'S," SAYS JOE, "HE WOULD MARINATE fresh freestone peaches in the summertime in a big jar with wine and maybe a little brandy. Then when his customers ordered dessert, he would put a jar of peaches on the table and let them help themselves. Sometimes that's all they wanted, other times they would spoon them over ice cream or a slice of sponge cake. This recipe for peaches in Italian sparkling wine reminds me of my father's peach dessert."

SERVES 4 TO 6

6 large, ripe peaches, peeled and thinly sliced

1 tablespoon sugar

8 ounces Asti Spumante sparkling wine

2 ounces crème de cassis liqueur

Place the peach slices in a large serving bowl. Add the sugar and toss gently. Add the Asti Spumante and crème de cassis, stir to combine, and refrigerate 4 to 6 hours before serving.

Red Buttons

"I first went to Patsy's during the war. That was the war between me and my ex-wife's divorce lawyer. I've been eating there ever since. I love their chopped liver, matzo ball soup, and the brisket of beef special. Naturally, I enjoyed them even more when Patsy picked up the check. I liked Patsy: He kissed my ring when I came in, and he was never indicted. I have to admit that I have a crush on the two lady cashiers: Anna DiCola, (Patsy's daughter) and Rose Scognamillo (Joe's wife). What I also appreciate about the folks at Patsy's is that they have a sense of humor. What I wrote here proves it. Oh yeah, my favorite dish? Porcelain!"

PEARS
POACHED WITH PEAR LIQUEUR

POACHED PEARS ARE A FAMILIAR IDEA, BUT THE ADDITION OF A PEAR liqueur makes it different enough to serve to guests. To ensure ripe pears for this dish, you may have to purchase them as much as a week in advance. Too often they're picked and shipped green.

SERVES 4

4 ripe, firm Bosc pears

¼ cup sugar

¼ cup pear liqueur

Core each pear from the bottom, leaving the stems intact, and cut a small slice from the bottom of each pear. Stand the pears in a small stovetop casserole.

Combine the sugar and liqueur with 2½ cups water in a medium bowl. Pour over the pears (the liquid should cover the bottom half of the pears). Bring the liquid to a boil over medium heat. Cover, reduce flame to low, and simmer for 25 minutes, or until the pears are tender. Using a slotted spoon, remove the pears from the liquid and reserve.

Cook the liquid until it is reduced to a thin syrup, about 8 to 10 minutes. Spoon the syrup over the pears and serve warm or at room temperature.

LEMON RICOTTA TORTE

THIS TORTE, PREPARED THE ITALIAN WAY WITH RICOTTA CHEESE, IS lighter than most American cheesecakes and can be served after a large dinner.

SERVES 8

1 3-pound container whole-milk ricotta cheese

1²/₃ cups sugar

3 extra-large eggs

½ teaspoon vanilla extract

Zest from 1 lemon

Butter and flour, for greasing pan

Preheat the oven to 400°F.

In a large bowl, mix the ricotta, sugar, eggs, vanilla, and lemon zest until well blended.

Butter and flour a 9 x 2-inch round baking pan. Spoon the ricotta mixture into the pan and smooth the top with a spatula. To avoid having rising batter spill over the side of the pan while baking, construct a "collar" to wrap around the pan, extending at least 2 inches above the pan's top edge. Construct the collar with a sheet of aluminum foil, folded in half lengthwise, inside surface greased, and secured with string or tape. Bake on the oven's bottom shelf for 55 minutes.

Refrigerate for 3 to 4 hours. Remove from refrigerator and allow to return to room temperature before serving.

ZABAGLIONE

FOREVER A FAVORITE IS THIS SIMPLE DESSERT WHIPPED UP WITH EGGS, sugar, and wine. I've added a touch of cinnamon, which gives a bit of color as well as flavor to this great old-fashioned dessert.

SERVES 4

6 egg yolks

½ cup sugar

⅓ cup sweet Marsala wine

½ teaspoon cinnamon

Combine the egg yolks, sugar, and wine in the top of a double boiler. Place over water that is just simmering and beat constantly. The mixture will first foam and then thicken. The zabaglione is ready to serve when the mixture holds a soft peak.

Sprinkle with cinnamon and serve immediately.

Joe Franklin

"Sure, I have my own restaurant, but I still go to Patsy's a lot," says Joe Franklin. "It's a habit I got into when I was a kid and I used to hang around Eddie Cantor. Remember him? A famous comedian on the stage and the radio. One day I went over to meet him at the Sherry-Netherland Hotel where he was staying, and there was another old-time star with him—the singer Al Jolson. It was a real thrill when they offered to take me to dinner. Where? At Patsy's. They loved the food, especially the bread, as I remember. I've been going there ever since. It's one of my better habits."

WALNUT-FILLED CREPES

WHETHER YOU CALL THEM PANCAKES, CREPES, OR *CRESPELLE* AS THEY DO in Italy, everybody likes this dessert. Crepes are really simple to prepare, but look very impressive. When you become adept at preparing them, you'll be able to work with two pans simultaneously without any trouble. A major advantage to a dessert of crepes is that they can be made in the morning and served at dinner. And leftover crepes (though that rarely happens) make a wonderful breakfast treat.

SERVES 6 TO 8

2 cups shelled walnut pieces

½ cup sugar

1 cup all-purpose flour

2 tablespoons sugar

3 large eggs

1½ cups milk

2 teaspoons grated lemon rind

⅛ teaspoon salt

Butter, for cooking crepes (about ¼ pound)

Combine the walnuts and sugar in a food processor and pulse until nuts are finely ground. Transfer the nut mixture to a bowl, and rinse out the processor bowl and blade.

Combine the flour, sugar, eggs, milk, lemon rind, and salt in the food processor and process until all ingredients are thoroughly blended. Transfer the mixture to a bowl or pitcher and refrigerate for 1 hour before using.

In a 6-inch nonstick skillet or omelet pan heat a small amount of the butter over medium flame. Using a small ladle, spoon enough batter into the pan to coat the bottom. Tilt the pan so that the batter spreads evenly. Cook over medium heat for 1 minute, or until the batter is set. Turn and cook on the second side until lightly brown, about 30 seconds. Slide the crepe out of the pan onto a flat platter and continue preparing crepes with remaining batter.

Allow the crepes to cool. Place 1 tablespoon of the nut mixture on top of each crepe and roll carefully. Place the filled crepes in a shallow baking pan or on a rimmed cookie sheet, cover with foil, and reserve until ready to serve. Before serving, warm the crepes in a preheated 350°F. oven for 5 to 7 minutes, or until heated through.

We Owe It All to . . .

"Why are we so popular?" says Anna. "I think because we have always followed my father's philosophy: 'Never say no to a customer.' I remember one night when we were getting ready to close and someone came in and wanted gnocchi. We were all out of gnocchi, but that didn't matter. My father told my brother, Joe, to go into the kitchen and prepare some more gnocchi. Today, if many of our customers want dishes that are not on the menu, we make it for them and add it to our menu.

"My father used to go around in this gray jacket—he didn't look like the owner of Patsy's, he looked like one of the hired help. He did this so he could lend a hand, clean off the tables if necessary, do everything. And when he served, he did it elegantly. He would bring a main dish out on a platter to present it to a guest, and after that he would transfer it to an individual plate.

"We learned to cater to our customers. One night Steve Ross showed up with a party of thirty people. He was the head of Time Warner, and he banged on the door and said, 'Joe, you gotta feed us. What am I going to do with all these people?' He had Robin Williams with him and Christopher Reeve, Dustin Hoffman—a whole bunch. It was after eleven and everyone in the kitchen had gone home. But Joe opened the door, went back in the kitchen, and cooked for everyone.

"That's why people are loyal to Patsy's. I remember one winter when there was a big snowstorm and we told the help to stay home. We weren't expecting many people, maybe just a few from the neighborhood. But sure enough, there were people from out of town who had reserved, and snow or no snow, they drove down. It took them hours, so of course we made them dinner."

ACKNOWLEDGMENTS

The job of a chef is challenging. . . . So was writing this cookbook. I'd like to thank the many people in my immediate and extended family who supported me in this project. First on the list are my grandparents, Pasquale (familiarly known as Patsy) and Concetta. They are the founders of our family here in the wonderful United States, and the founders of Patsy's Italian Restaurant. I knew my grandfather better, as he outlived my grandmother and passed away when I was in my twenties. I was at his side helping out at the restaurant from the time I was a kid. I would see him often, even after he retired, because he would come into the restaurant frequently to check us out—making sure that we were doing things the right way, that the high quality of the food, cooking, and service that he had originated had not changed.

My grandfather was pleased when I decided to become part of Patsy's. I learned to cook at my father's side, just as my father had learned from Patsy. When I started out in the restaurant's kitchen, my father, Joe, said, "Sal, now I'm the chef and you're my apprentice, but there will come a time when you'll be the chef and I'll be the apprentice." My father, my mother, Rose, my aunt Anna DiCola, and her son, my cousin Frank DiCola, are the people in the front of the restaurant now that I'm the chef. They keep the world of Patsy's running smoothly.

My father is the reason Patsy's is here today. He's worked here all of his life, and continues to do so. That deserves special gratitute—thanks, Dad! And Mom, you have always been there for me. Thanks. Let me add that my cousin Frank is more like a brother than a cousin. He does his best to keep me sane when problems—and there are always problems in the restaurant business—pile up. ("What do you mean, the vegetable order hasn't arrived?" "I ordered twenty veal chops, not ten!")

My wife and children deserve recognition for their patience and understanding of the 24/7 life of a chef and restaurant owner. They are my strength.

Now let me talk about my extended restaurant family. There's Michele Pascetta, who tirelessly takes care of all the myriad details of a restaurant's office. Russ Cahill, who found his way to Patsy's from Ohio and has been with us since 1989 as our in-house director of advertising and marketing. And Susan Angrisani, who handles the important business of selling our sauces and other products. She and Russ have helped put our sauces on supermarket shelves around the country. Let me mention here that we originally went into the sauce business at the suggestion of many of our customers—a great idea. Thank you.

My immediate family and I recognize that our terrific kitchen help and our wonderful wait staff do a lot to make Patsy's a home away from home to our customers. I don't have room to include all their names, but a special salute goes to our elegant captains, Vinnie and Pino, who do so much to keep our guests happy, and to Mendoza, who has been with us for more than thirty years, ensuring that all our deliveries are in perfect order. Thanks also to Aubrey Reuben, who provided many of the photos used in this book, and to George Kalinsky for his photograph of Frank Sinatra.

I'd like to tell all the people I've met in publishing that I now consider them part of my extended family. There's my editor, Chris Pavone, whose hard work and guidance made this book so special. And Carmel Berman Reingold, without whose help and keen eye to detail this book would have never materialized. Thanks as well to the folks at Clarkson Potter and Random House, especially Chip Gibson, Andrew Martin, Don Weisberg, Madeline McIntosh, Barbara Marks, Katie Workman, Lauren Shakely, John Groton, Joan DeMayo, Andrea Rosen, Pam Krauss, and Leigh Ann Ambrosi. Thanks to Jane Treuhaft for the wonderful design, and to Camille Smith for attending to an incredible breadth of details. And very special greetings to my friend Rich Romano. Rich has been a part of my extended family for many years—we went to school together when we were kids. Rich has been saying for years that I could write a book and that Patsy's Restaurant deserved one. I'm happy and grateful to say that he was right on both counts.

And I want to express very special thanks to the two people who offered encouragement every step of the way—Frank's daughter, Nancy Sinatra, and Rush Limbaugh. Do I have a big family or what? And are they great? You bet!

INDEX

CONVERSION CHART

EQUIVALENT IMPERIAL AND METRIC MEASUREMENTS

American cooks use standard containers, the 8-ounce cup and a tablespoon that takes exactly 16 level fillings to fill that cup level. Measuring by cup makes it very difficult to give weight equivalents, as a cup of densely packed butter will weigh considerably more than a cup of flour. The easiest way therefore to deal with cup measurements in recipes is to take the amount by volume rather than by weight. Thus the equation reads:

1 cup = 240 ml = 8 fl. oz.   1/2 cup = 120 ml = 4 fl. oz.

In the States, butter is often measured in sticks. One stick is the equivalent of 8 tablespoons. One tablespoon of butter is therefore the equivalent to ½ ounce or 15 grams.

LIQUID MEASURES

Fluid Ounces	U.S.	Imperial	Milliliters
	1 teaspoon	1 teaspoon	5
¼	2 teaspoons	1 dessertspoon	10
½	1 tablespoon	1 tablespoon	14
1	2 tablespoons	2 tablespoons	28
2	¼ cup	4 tablespoons	56
4	½ cup		120
5		¼ pint or 1 gill	140
6	¾ cup		170
8	1 cup		240
9			250, ¼ liter
10	1¼ cups	½ pint	280
12	1½ cups		340
15		¾ pint	420
16	2 cups		450
18	2¼ cups		500, ½ liter
20	2½ cups	1 pint	560
24	3 cups		675
25		1¼ pints	700
27	3½ cups		750
30	3¾ cups	1½ pints	840
32	4 cups or 1 quart		900
35		1¾ pints	980
36	4½ cups		1000, 1 liter
40	5 cups	2 pints or 1 quart	1120

SOLID MEASURES

U.S. and Imperial Measures		Metric Measures	
Ounces	Pounds	Grams	Kilos
1		28	
2		56	
3½		100	
4	¼	112	
5		140	
6		168	
8	½	225	
9		250	¼
12	¾	340	
16	1	450	
18		500	½
20	1¼	560	
24	1½	675	
27		750	¾
28	1¾	780	
32	2	900	
36	2¼	1000	1
40	2½	1100	
48	3	1350	
54		1500	1½

OVEN TEMPERATURE EQUIVALENTS

Fahrenheit	Celsius	Gas Mark	Description
225	110	¼	Cool
250	130	½	
275	140	1	Very Slow
300	150	2	
325	170	3	Slow
350	180	4	Moderate
375	190	5	
400	200	6	Moderately Hot
425	220	7	Fairly Hot
450	230	8	Hot
475	240	9	Very Hot
500	250	10	Extremely Hot

Any broiling recipes can be used with the grill of the oven, but beware of high-temperature grills.

EQUIVALENTS FOR INGREDIENTS

all-purpose flour—plain flour
baking sheet—oven tray
buttermilk—ordinary milk
cheesecloth—muslin
coarse salt—kitchen salt
cornstarch—cornflour
eggplant—aubergine

granulated sugar—caster sugar
half and half—12% fat milk
heavy cream—double cream
light cream—single cream
lima beans—broad beans
parchment paper—greaseproof paper
plastic wrap—cling film

scallion—spring onion
shortening—white fat
unbleached flour—strong, white flour
vanilla bean—vanilla pod
zest—rind
zucchini—courgettes or marrow

PATSY'S *Sauces*

Now that you know about our restaurant, let me tell you about our bottled sauces. We started making them a few years ago because so many of our customers asked for them. They wanted to make a quick but delicious meal at home, and they would often ask us for "a little sauce to take out." That gave us the idea to bottle some of the favorites. Easier said than done. We had to work out the recipes, find someone to follow those recipes, and above all make sure that anything with the Patsy's name on it was of a consistently high quality.

It took us a while, but we finally did it. Today we're proud to offer seven sauces that follow the recipes used in our kitchen. When the jarred sauces were tested against those brought directly from our restaurant kitchen, the Food Network stated they could find no differences in flavor or quality. In competitions across the country, these sauces have won a multitude of awards. We use the best ingredients, whether the sauces are prepared at the restaurant or for bottling. Our sauces are labor-intensive—for example, the basil and garlic are hand cut. And while some bottlers prepare one huge batch of sauce and hope for the best, we make our sauces in very small batches, and taste test every one.

MARINARA—the mother sauce. It includes tomatoes, olive oil, onions, basil, parsley, garlic, and just a touch of oregano.

TOMATO BASIL—made with chunks of tomatoes, lots of onions, plenty of basil, and a bouquet of spices. It contains no garlic and differs from Marinara because of the larger quantity of onions and basil.

FRA DIAVOLO—for those who like a tang of hot spice. This sauce contains a mix of tomatoes, garlic, parsley, onions, a touch of basil, and a good-size kick from the crushed red pepper flakes.

PUTTANESCA—a sauce that starts out innocently with tomatoes, basil, garlic, herbs and spices, and then goes wild with olives, capers, and anchovies.

VODKA—a light, delicate tomato sauce, gently spiced, with a touch of vodka and made velvety with cream.

AMATRICIANA—it all begins with tomatoes, and then this sauce is made truly interesting with bacon, prosciutto, onions, and basil.

PIZZAIOLA—the garlic for this sauce is sautéed in olive oil, to which are added tomatoes, roasted red peppers, mushrooms, parsley, a touch of oregano, salt, and pepper.

Our sauces are sold throughout the United States at better grocers and specialty food stores. And at 1-800-3-PATSYS (1-800-372-8797). You can contact us at www.patsys.com.

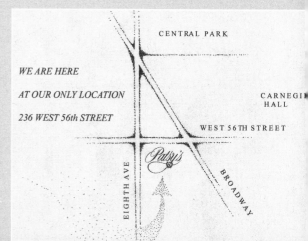

WE ARE HERE
AT OUR ONLY LOCATION
236 WEST 56th STREET

CENTRAL PARK

CARNEGIE HALL

WEST 56TH STREET

Patsy's

EIGHTH AVE

BROADWAY